Dedicated to:

My dad

A master storyteller. He taught me the gospel through stories.

My mom

She makes me believe I can do anything.

My husband

My rock and my true love.

My kids

You are my stories and my greatest blessings.

I only went out for a walk,
And finally concluded
To stay out till sundown,
For going out,
I found
Was really
Going
In.

John Muir

TABLE OF CONTENTS

Introduction

Go Get 'Em

It was 6:00 a.m. when I heard the click of my alarm. I reached over and turned it off. The alarm was set so I could get up and down the mountain before the heat of the day set in. The night before I had promised myself that I would get up and do my early morning hike to start the day right. From years of exercise, I'm pretty fit for 53 years of age. Most people don't understand that physical fitness isn't what really compels me to get up and down the mountain. It's a mental fitness that I'm after.

My close friends know depression and anxiety runs deep in my family roots. My Grandpa Cederlof had it before it had a label. It was "he's just not feeling well." I think about how lonely and helpless he must have felt during the years that depression got control of him.

I got slammed with depression shortly after my first child was born. I was working full time with a child in full-time day care and supporting our family while my husband set his sights on three years of law school. There had been other times in my life when I felt depleted, worn out and pulled in too many directions and was barely able to keep my head above water. This time I sunk. I sunk into a dark and lonely place where hope does not exist.

A place where it is a desperate attempt to make it through a single day.

A place where you just want it all to end.

A place where I'd go to the bathroom stall several times a day at work and scream and cry in complete silence.

1

A place where I'd put my child in her crib for a nap on the weekends and crawl under the crib into the dark corner and lay there in the fetal position until she woke up.

A place I never want to return to.

And so I hike. The endorphins and the fresh air and the sunshine feed my soul. I'm one step ahead, one hike ahead, one mountain ahead of the devastating disease of depression. It's a race that I'm winning. The physical fitness of my body is just a nice side effect of exercising. Positivity in my thoughts – that's what I'm really after.

This particular morning my legs felt heavy and tired as I turned off the alarm. Maybe I'll hike in the afternoon – sleep in a bit and deal with the heat later. But I knew better. So I jumped up, threw my workout clothes on and drove to the mountain trail. As I walked toward the trail, I silently prayed to Heavenly Father about what the Spirit had been telling me for years – write a book. I needed courage to begin. Lately the message I was feeling and hearing in my mind and heart had an urgency to it. I needed to gather my thoughts and my courage and begin writing this book that was somehow important and necessary. "Please Heavenly Father – give me courage … "

I felt the familiar exertion of leg muscles pulling me up the start of the climb and the direct effect it had on my lungs. This is where I needed to be. I saw a group of three men on the trail headed toward me. They had clearly hiked an hour earlier and were now headed down the mountain. I pulled my head up to nod the casual "good morning" greeting that we hikers do. One of the men caught my attention. He looked me directly in the eye and said, "Go get 'em."

Go get 'em. It was a direct answer to my prayer and I knew it.

I thought about those words all the way up the mountain. *Go get 'em.* They were words of encouragement. Positive words. Words that implied that it could be done. A message to me about having the courage and dedication to write, to love, to teach and to share my experiences and testimony. Clearly the hiker was referring to the immediate situation of pulling my body up the side of a mountain. Nature's elements are all around waiting to be conquered. Narrow rocky trails, cactus and rattlesnakes there to keep my attention focused. *Go get 'em.* A tender mercy on the mountain just for me.

Go get 'em. I thought of them on a larger scale – an eternal scale. Perhaps Heavenly Father looked us directly in the eye and said something similar. Words of encouragement. Positive words. Words that implied that it could be done. In His infinite wisdom he knew we would have steep, rocky trails to climb here on Earth. He knew there would be sweat and tears and pain. He also knew that it was all part of a beautiful plan. A Plan of Salvation. A Plan of Redemption. A Plan of Mercy. A Plan of Happiness. A Plan which would bring His children up the difficult trails of life, but ultimately bring them back down the mountain toward home – our eternal home. And He knew we could do it.

And so I write. My experiences and my trials are no doubt different from yours. The common experience we all share in this life is pain. Physical pain. Emotional pain. Pain that literally hurts your heart.

But this is not a book about trials. This is a book about hope. It is about seeing and hearing and feeling and looking for hope despite the pain and worry that consumes you. It is positioning your heart, mind and soul to recognize the messages of hope from God.

There are three reasons we all encounter painful trials: consequence to a choice, mortality (a physical nature) and lessons we are to learn. Regardless of which reason we find ourselves struggling, the way to handle it is the same. It is why we are here – to become closer to God through it. To become like Him. We are to take a stumbling block and figure out how to make it a stepping stone. Because life doesn't happen TO you – it happens FOR you.

Though our trials may be different, I have discovered a spiritual pattern which takes the focus off of our feet plodding up the trail – a pattern which gives us strength as we pull ourselves and our gaze upward. Thought processes and patterns in our daily lives which allow us to feel hope in what feels like an impossible storm. Hope replacing fear. An eternal perspective. That is something that we can all cling to on this hike we call life.

Chapter 1

I Am a Child of God

It was a beautiful day in Park City, Utah. The sun was shining, the air was clear and the July wild flowers were blooming. There could be no better place or day for a hike. The kids and grandkids were all gathered together for one of our many summer adventures. We were headed for a beautiful little lake where we would have a picnic lunch. My three daughters were there along with two little grandsons at about one year of age. I had Tucker on my back and my husband had Quinn on his. My son, Austin, was at the Missionary Training Center in Provo, Utah, where he was preparing to serve a mission for the Church of Jesus Christ of Latter-day Saints in Russia. He had been there for 11 weeks learning the Russian language. In another week he would leave for Novosibirsk. Life was good and I knew it.

As I walked along the hiking trail, I felt blessed. The smell of the pines brought a sense of serenity to my soul. The sight of the green landscape and the majestic mountains of Park City surrounding me was not unnoticed. I am used to the beauty of the Arizona desert so this was a visual delight. Tucker's little feet were bouncing along as he sat in the pack on my back. The lake was just another half mile or so down the trail.

I stopped to check on the progress of the others on the trail behind me. We were happy and laughing and enjoying our time together. What a great day. It was then that the voice spoke to me. It was a voice that I heard in my mind above all the laughter and the sounds of nature. It was a voice that shook me to the core. The message was clear – *"be grateful for what you have because it's going to change.*" I recognized it as truth. I recognized the Spirit. My heart sank.

I immediately began to pray. I began to list the blessings of my life. There was not a friend or family member forgotten. For the next half mile on the trail I offered prayers of gratitude for the love and happiness in my life. They were prayers of the heart. I poured my soul out to God hoping to recognize all and not leave anything or anyone out.

At the lake we threw sticks in the water. The dogs jumped in to fetch the sticks and the grandchildren giggled at the sight. We found some large rocks and sat by the lake to rest. I couldn't even speak of the message. I looked around at my three daughters and clung to the grandchildren in my arms. I thought of Austin in the MTC. I looked at my husband as he dug snacks out of his pack. Whose life would be affected? What? How? So many questions.

As we hiked back out of the canyon, I began to argue with myself. Maybe I hadn't really heard anything. Perhaps it was just a strange, random thought that meant nothing. I would not speak of it to anyone. How could I? My spirit recognized it as a merciful message, but my mortal mind would push it back and hope that nothing came of it. A quiet fear crept in and consumed a corner of my heart.

Two days later we received the phone call. "Please come to the Mission Training Center and pick up your son. He will not be traveling to Russia." To say that my heart sank wouldn't even suffice. I had never before felt the pain of a broken heart. My heart was broken for him. It ached within my chest. He had talked of serving a mission his entire life. It was his purpose. It was his destiny. It was my purpose – to raise a son with a testimony and desire to serve others. It was my destiny – to be a missionary mom.

Obviously this was a huge trial for Austin. Despite incredible pressures and expectations, he was honest with himself and God and knew that he wasn't ready. He made the right decision. I knew it and was proud of him. He has always had a tender and true heart. It's what I admire most about him. He spoke with truth and love for the Savior. He understood the Atonement and was grateful for the miracles and mercies of the MTC experience. It was the hardest and best thing he's ever done.

I am a child of God …

You might say why was this a trial for me? Raw emotion and a sudden shift in my perfectly planned path rocked me. I had fed missionaries in my home for the past 19 years. In our vacation travels, I frequently saw missionaries all over the world. I always stopped them and honored their service. I took pictures and wrote letters to their mothers to let them know that their sons were healthy and happy. My love for missionaries has been strong and heartfelt my entire life. I was going to be a missionary mom one day. And I wanted the best for my son.

"If only" questions consumed me. I second-guessed every decision and situation in raising him over the past 19 years. If only we had read more scriptures. If only we had prayed more as a family. If only we hadn't skipped some Family Home Evenings. If only I had been a better mother. The family's emotions were raw and pushed to the limit. My marriage relationship was tested, my self-esteem was tested and my faith was tested.

I thought back to the message on the hike. That beautifully horrible message. I quickly recognized it as one of the greatest tender mercies I had ever received. I clung to that message because of the truth behind it. Not the truth that things were going to change – I certainly was living and breathing and crawling through that. The truth that Heavenly Father knew me. And I knew that He knew my son. What a tender mercy for me. Currently there are 7 billion people on Earth and yet my family mattered. In all the difficulties that lay ahead with doubts and seemingly unanswered prayers, I wrapped both arms around it and clung to that mercy and to that knowledge. I knew I was a child of God and I knew that He loved me.

And He has sent me here …

This life and many of the difficulties and trials which would await was probably no surprise to us in the pre-earth life. We had an understanding of the purpose for our field trip to Earth. For God *"made these things known unto us … yea, and he has made these things known unto us beforehand, because he loveth our souls … "* (Alma 24:14).

Today He has full confidence in us because He knew us before we came here. We learn in Jeremiah that *"before I formed thee in the belly I knew thee … "* (Jeremiah 1:5). He knows our strengths and our weaknesses and knows exactly which trails are meant for us. Trails that will test our limits.

I like to think of life as a culmination of hikes. There are easy trails – rolling trails with wildflowers along the path. Trails with little exertion required. Trails where the beauty of life is seen and recognized and felt. These are blessed days. These are the days when we catch our breath and feel the beauty and the love and the majesty of life.

There are moderate trails and trails that take increased effort. The glimpses of beauty along the path are not constant. It's the hike with the annoying rock in your shoe. You can deal with it, but it is a bit uncomfortable. We trudge upward and only occasionally stop to recognize flowers blooming. Our focus is more intent on the endurance of the hike. We have thoughts like, "How much longer?" and in steeper sections silently wish for the end.

And then there are those dark, steep and seemingly never-ending difficult trails. These trails test our endurance. We may think we have packed all essential supplies for this hike, but it hits so hard and fast that at once we feel unprepared and intimidated. We are not physically or mentally ready. This is where fear rushes in while hopes dash away. We can easily lose our way on these trails. Negativity can reach in and rob our bodies and minds of all possibilities of success. Cliffs appear to be pulling us to the edge. The steepness of the elevation robs our lungs of air and makes our heart pound and ache. We may have had brief encounters with difficult trails before, but each new difficult hike brings with it a gut-wrenching panic that can consume us. These are the days when we cannot see the wild flowers along our difficult path. We keep our head and our gaze down just trying to put one foot in front of the other. These are days of discouragement and despair. Days when we cannot see the end.

When we're on a moderate or difficult trail in life it is easy to ask, "Why me?" It's the immediate knee-jerk reaction. If we think about the Plan of Salvation and all the blessings that ultimately come from it, we wouldn't ever ask. Our mortal screams NO but our spirit says YES! Perhaps our spirits are shouting yes because they remember that one big reason we came here was to grow. Tough situations and life's trials are the catalyst which begins that process.

"For behold, this life is the time for men to prepare to meet God ... " (Alma 34:32).

Part of the preparation for meeting God is to become more like Him. We become more like Him through experiencing trials and allowing that difficulty to expose raw emotion. That raw emotion will show itself in some form. Will we be angry? Will we be sad? Will we be disappointed? Will we lose hope? The answer is yes – all of the above. The real test is taking that emotion, feeling it, recognizing and ultimately turning it over to the Lord for help. It is humility in the truest emotional sense. Moving away from the "why me" to "what now." It is turning over what we feel and all the unfairness of it to the Lord and having faith that He knows best.

In this act of humility the Lord will take our tears, our despair, our heartaches and our weaknesses and make them strong. Let's put some perspective on this. Before we learn how our weaknesses can be made strong, let's remember where our weaknesses came from. God knows us and he knew us before we came here.

"And if men come unto me I will show unto them their weakness. I give unto men weakness that they may be humble ... " (Ether 12:27).

Hartman Rector Jr. stated, "Where do you suppose we get these weaknesses? If you pose this question to a group of Saints, it will astound you how many different answers you get to this particular question. Some will say that they are responsible for their own weaknesses; well, if you keep your weaknesses, that's true, but that is not where they come from. Another will say weaknesses come from heredity or environment. ... So where do we get our weaknesses? We get them from the Lord; the Lord gives us weaknesses so we will be humble. This makes us teachable."[1]

God knows that our weaknesses are a conduit to this inspired process of becoming stronger. That is what makes the Plan beautiful. It doesn't feel beautiful in the process, but from an eternal perspective it is. We are becoming more like God. This promised equation of weakness = future strength is found in the second half of Ether 12:27:

"For if they humble themselves before me, and have faith in me, then will I make weak things become strong unto them."

This is a promise from the Lord – hinging on our faith. We can be changed, molded and formed into a strength and a source of power to those whom we serve and love. It is understanding that God's plan is not to give you peace *from* the storm, but to give you peace *during* the storm. To believe that good, strong members of the church who righteously follow the commandments are safe from storms is not fully understanding the mission of our life here. The storms and difficult hikes take our weaknesses and lay them out on the table of life before us. This is the chance to fall down, get back up again and gain strength in the process. We signed up to fall down. Sometimes it's scabbed knees. Sometimes it's a face plant. It is difficult. But it is necessary. It is the Plan.

And so my needs are great ...

As I hiked in the Park City mountains for weeks after Austin returned home from the MTC, I longed for an eternal perspective. I longed for peace. My heart ached and despair had taken over my spirit. I needed a healthy perspective for several reasons. Trials and difficulties can take center stage in one's life and stretch limits of patience and faith. We've all known family and friends whose testimony and commitment to the gospel crumbles under the weight. I didn't want to be one of those statistics. Doubts of God's love and fairness were swirling in my thoughts. Years of gospel study and understanding allowed me to see with some clarity what was happening. This trail felt slippery. I clung with all my might to my faith.

Five and 10-mile hikes became an almost daily requirement. I craved it. It was a way for me to fight through it. The more difficult the hiking conditions the better. Somehow I hoped that I could leave my negative energy on the mountain. Prayers during this emotionally raw time were begging and pleading. My heart knew that Heavenly Father knew what was best for our family, but my head wanted to be in control. I felt I knew what was best! Fear was overtaking faith.

My thoughts turned toward gospel truths I'd been taught as a child. When negative and tragic "what ifs" began to take control of my thoughts, I clung to these truths that were deep in my soul.

Help me to understand His words, before it grows too late ...

As I hiked, that beautiful and familiar song became my anchor. It grounded me when negative thoughts wanted to take me elsewhere. Over and over again I would repeat and consider the meaning behind all three verses of *"I Am A Child of God."* [2]

Rich blessings are in store ...

If I but learn to do His will, I'll live with Him once more ...

The beauty and the simplicity of the lyrics were calming. They are simple, yet profound. I wondered as I sang them again and again on my hikes if Primary children ever really understood the power of the words they were singing. To this day the song brings tender memories to my mind and tears to my eyes. The song expresses the circle of life. It is a beautiful representation of the Plan.

Lead me guide me ... walk beside me

One particular day on a long, emotionally wrenching hike, I was overcome with feelings of hopelessness. I felt my prayers for Austin's mission had not been answered. Life felt as though it was spinning out of my control. I had lost my purpose. Hope was lost. As I forged my way up the mountainside, I felt lost in the world. Life was too hard. Tears streamed down my face as sorrow overwhelmed my emotions and my energy. I prayed with a fervent, desperate cry to God. Did I even matter?

Just then, dozens of butterflies surrounded me, swirling around me for five minutes as I pushed forward. Encircled by beautiful, white butterflies. A tender mercy from God. My broken heart recognized it. I mattered. God knew who I was and what I was feeling. My son mattered. We all matter. God knows and loves each of us individually. A simple sign. I am a child of God. And He walked beside me that day. There is no doubt.

Chapter 2

Seek Me Diligently

To say it was unexpected is putting it mildly. My daughter Aubreigh was busy with her oldest son Quinn and new baby Bennett. She had her hands full. Life at this stage with little ones is just getting through each day with your sanity intact. Sometimes getting out of your pajamas and into clothes is a benchmark for success. Her husband, Matt, ignored the sleep deprivation of life since the baby was born and headed out to the office like it was any ordinary day. Life was good. A new home and two adorable kids.

But this would be no ordinary day. When Matt walked into the office he could not have predicted the news. Layoffs. His department had been eliminated. Apologies were made. The company was in trouble. Pack your things and good luck.

Matt called Aubreigh. "I'm coming home early – and not going back." Aubreigh hung up and called me. I tried to find the silver lining. Consciously calming my voice I searched for optimistic words of encouragement. "We'll make a plan. A rescue plan. I'll call my family and friends. Certainly someone will know of a job opening. It's a tough economy, but Matt is talented and we can do this."

Immediately fears push forward and what-ifs dominate thoughts. What if we have to leave our house, our friends. What if Matt can't find any work? How will we make our house payment? Do we have enough food storage? How will I buy diapers?

We all pulled together as a family support system. We would fix this.

Phone calls were made. Resume and cover letters were rapidly updated. We can tackle this. We will do everything in our power to push through this. It was hugs and encouraging words for Matt. "Don't worry – it will be okay."

Somebody noticed as we rushed around changing the world, trying to alter the course of things. Somebody noticed a somber mood in the house. Somebody clearly overheard conversations and felt the fear. That somebody was 3-year-old Quinn.

It was about three days into the job-loss situation. Aubreigh was getting ready to tuck Quinn in for bed. He had been taught by his good parents about prayer. Bedtime prayers every night.

"Heavenly Father – thank you for my Mommy, Daddy and baby Bennett. Thank you for my tractors and my big dump truck. Please help me to find a job for Daddy. In the name of Jesus Christ, Amen."

Aubreigh's heart sank. In all our well-intentioned efforts did we ever pause to ask for divine help? If a 3-year-old believes in his little tender heart that he can ask Heavenly Father to help him with a task, shouldn't we as well? What pure and simple faith. "As soon as we learn the true relationship in which we stand toward God (namely, God is our Father, and we are his children), then at once prayer becomes natural and instinctive on our part."[1] Quinn had begun to understand this. It was natural for him to ask for his Heavenly Father's help. Daddy did find a new job and perhaps that blessing is due in part to a little 3-year-old boy's faith.

Maybe we forget that important father-child relationship with God as we grow up and become independent and self-reliant. As parents we have within us a burning desire to convey some of life's meaning to our youngsters. Wouldn't we like to instill in them insight to foresee some of life's pitfalls? To give them warning. To spare them some of the unhappiness that we have known because of ignorance or impatience or weakness.[2] As children we look to authority for many of life's decisions through earthly parents and our heavenly parents. It is the natural order of things.

We grow up to become independent of our earthly parents by becoming responsible and capable of making mature decisions. As life moves forward it is easy to celebrate our own achievements and neglect our communication with our Heavenly Father. Life gets complicated and prayers become an afterthought. Our conversations with Heavenly Father can become routine and repetitive. It's time to evaluate our conversations with Him.

We have much to learn from little children as they speak with simple and heartfelt words. They are perhaps the greatest teachers of all. *"Whosoever therefore shall humble himself as this little child, the same is greatest in the kingdom of heaven"* (Matthew 18:4).

My parents taught me very early about prayer. *"And they shall also teach their children to pray, and to walk uprightly before the Lord"* (D&C 68:28). I have tender childhood memories of Dad kneeling by our bedsides as we conversed with God each night. My Heavenly Father heard those prayers. So did my earthly father. Fortunately on those nights when Dad's heart was particularly touched by sincere words, he kissed us goodnight then wandered back to his den where he pulled out a notebook and recorded those conversations:

- We had recently had our dog Punch put to sleep. "Thank you for Punch. Help us to all die and see Punch and help Punch that she'll have lots of dogs to play with and they'll be nice to her."

- To our new dog Dusty. "Bless Dusty to find some friends so she won't be lonely while we are at school."

- "I'm thankful that there are no monsters at our house."

- "Help the boys and girls at school to be nice to the boy who had his face operated on so they won't laugh at him."

- "Bless the pretty flowers to grow and that people won't mash them with their Hondas."

- "Help the children without mommies and daddies that someone will love them."

- "Bless the boys and girls without mommies that they can find something to eat and that they'll have clean panties in the mornings."

- "Bless the new plants to grow because Daddy's back hurts."

- And this to the children next door. "Bless the Stevens children to have a happy Christmas even when they don't believe in Christmas."

Children look at the situation plainly and directly ask God to help. Often as adults, our conversation with the Lord is much too general. There are seldom clichés in children's prayers. I remember well a scene on a stormy night which illustrates.

For a time, my dad was involved in mountain rescue and was often called out when people either fell or were stranded. On one terribly cold November night, the police called him because people were stranded on Camelback Mountain in Phoenix, Arizona. Rain was pouring. My Dad and his rescue partner struggled up the mountain with water running off in their faces. The rocks were slippery and dangerous and they both feared falling several hundred feet if footing was lost. After several hours they were able to find the stranded climbers, lower them with ropes, and finally climb down themselves. Dad was soaked, muddy and exhausted.

What Dad didn't know was that we were there at the mountain waiting for him. My mom was worried about the conditions of the rescue. Camelback Mountain was not too far from the house. She woke us up and told us to get into the car. We were going to go wait and pray for Dad. Rain pounded on the roof of the car. All six of us kids pressed our faces to the car windows trying to follow the lights on the mountain barely seen through sheets of water. Waiting for Dad. Praying for Dad.

When he made it back down the mountain he found the police captain. As my dad talked with him, he noticed – away from all the activity – his Volvo station wagon. He walked over to the car and we rolled the windows down, "Dad! We have been here all night praying for you! We prayed that your feet wouldn't slip on the rocks and that you could see in the dark and that you wouldn't fall!" No clichés. Simple heartfelt requests needed for the situation at hand. Children praying not just that Dad would be safe, but voicing the critical elements of his safety. Indeed, the Lord heard us that night.

Jesus – The Perfect Example

Did Jesus ever ask for help? We learn in the scriptures that he absolutely did. He was a perfect example of understanding and remembering and honoring that father-child relationship. Think about the trials in Jesus' life which caused Him to reach out in prayer to His Father. The Garden. The Cross. His visit with the Nephites. Many times the followers of Jesus couldn't find Him. They would go looking for Him. They would find Him "aside" as the scriptures say. Even the Savior took the time to step aside and ask his Father for help.

"We, if it was necessary for Him, our Lord, to have divine assistance, will find it all the more important to receive His assistance. And in every circumstance and condition surrounding the Latter-day Saints, while in the

performance of their duties, they are entitled to supernatural aid from the Holy Spirit, to help in the various conditions surrounding them, and in the duties that they are required to perform. The sacrifices that are required of us are of that nature that no man or woman could make them, unless aided by a supernatural power; and the Lord, in proposing these conditions, never intended that his people should ever be required to comply with them unless by supernatural aid, and of that kind that is not professed by any other class of religious people. He has promised this aid."[3]

When the Plan was designed and we left the presence of our Heavenly Father it was never His intention to abandon us. It was never "good luck – hope you find your way back." He expects and wants us to ask for help on this journey of life.

"Then shall ye call upon me, and ye shall go and pray unto me, and I will hearken unto you. And ye shall seek me, and find me, when ye shall search for me with all your heart" (Jeremiah 29:12-13).

Mutual Influence

How do we search and pray with all our heart? How do we pray so that we can be sure that God knows the desires of our soul? It is communicating with the Lord – not telling Him. I've raised four children and know from experience that we have many opportunities to communicate with our children all that we wish them to know. Notice that I said communicate – not tell. If we tell them, then we have a monologue and they won't remember it and may not even be interested in what they hear. You've all seen the glazed look in the eyes and the invisible shield that lowers itself between your voice and their interest. You have been shut down.

If we have a dialogue, or a two-way experience, it will be satisfying and important to both us and God. There will be meaning and mutual interest and influence. Here the environment between child and parent is workable. Both child and parent feel validated and teachable. This same communication can be present between us and our Heavenly Father. This two-way process takes place when we have a genuine and a real interest in the things that He is interested in. It is mutual understanding. It is being open and honest with ourselves and our Heavenly Father so that we can distinguish between a self-voice of doubt or fear or hope – or whatever it may be – and His voice.

True communication results in mutual influence. When people truly understand each other then they respond and can be influenced by each other. It is the same with our Heavenly Father. It is talking with our Heavenly Father in words and emotions and thoughts that are way beyond the standard scripts. *"But when ye pray, use not vain repetitions, as the heathen, for they think that they shall be heard for their much speaking"* (3 Nephi 13:7).

It is trusting Him enough to speak and deliver from the heart and also trusting and opening up your heart to receive His response. This is a two-way experience. This is mutual influence with your Heavenly Father. How often do we pray to get? If our prayers are routine and only a dose of the same "getting" prayers then we are not fulfilling our half of true communication. Instead of praying to get, how often do we ask:

- Help me to have the vision, the grace, the patience to see Thy will for me.
- Help me to see your intention.
- Help me to see my purpose. Help me to find my path.

Can your communication with the Lord result in mutual influence? Yes. The Lord's behavior is influenced. The scriptures point out over and over that He works with us according to the level of our faith. If we have a high level of faith, we become just that much better – a willing servant with whom He can work and whom He can use to serve His divine purposes. Our belief, trust, faith, as well as our doings and actions, influence

His behavior toward us.

The crucial dimension is the relationship. Communication is not so much a matter of words as it is of relationships.

All of us have been in situations with others where there is a strain. We are not sure where we stand – afraid that we might say the wrong thing. That we might offend or cause a scene. That there might be mis-understandings. Now think about those relationships with others that are meaningful and harmonious. We can communicate without words.

Prayer is the soul's sincere desire
Uttered or unexpressed
The motion of a hidden fire
That trembles in the breast.

Prayer is the burden of a sigh
The falling of a tear
The upward glancing of an eye
When none but God is near.[4]

Communicating without words comes from being together, talking, working, respecting, loving. The same is true of our relationship with our Father. The great King Benjamin of the Book of Mormon said,

"For how knoweth a man the master whom he has not served, and who is a stranger unto him, and is far from the thoughts and intents of his heart?" (Mosiah 5:13)

The Bible Dictionary states: "Prayer is the act by which the will of the Father and the will of the child are brought into correspondence with each other. The object of prayer is not to change the will of God, but to secure for ourselves and for others blessings that God is already willing to grant, but that are made conditional on our asking for them. Blessings require some work or effort on our part before we can obtain them. Prayer is a form of work, and is an appointed means for obtaining the highest of all blessings."[5]

Think of your relationship with God. Do we abide with Him? The dictionary defines "abide" as to remain, to stay, to continue in a particular condition, attitude or relationship.[6] Understanding that definition gives deeper meaning to words found in the New Testament:

"If ye abide in me, and my words abide in you, ye shall ask what ye will, and it shall be done unto you" (John 15:7).

Learning to abide in Him is a process not an event. We will spend a lifetime falling down, getting up and talking to our Heavenly Father about it. Some of those hiking trails in life are steeper than others and it becomes easy for our desperate voice to want to tell Heavenly Father what He needs to do for us.

For weeks, maybe months after Austin returned home from the MTC, I strongly suggested to Heavenly Father that He reach His divine hand down and place him back on the mission. I could think of no other option. Prayers were desperate and one-sided. I prayed that same prayer over and over again. I backed myself into a spiritual corner of confusion, mourning a lost opportunity for him. Fear of his future took a firm hold on my heart and blocked my faith in His answer. My relationship with God was shaken and two-way communication was blocked.

I never even considered that Austin might be learning something that Heavenly Father knew was critical and specific to Austin. There was a plan for him. A hike designed for him. I also never considered that I might need to learn something as well. Perhaps my hiking trail was to take me in a different direction. A path that would teach me something new.

Slowly my prayers began to change. My faith turned a corner. I knew that Heavenly Father knew every pain and joy and desire of my heart because I had told Him over and over. Now I felt a stirring which told me to love and let go. Austin, too, was finding his own way and his communication with his Heavenly Father was taken to another level. In separate ends of the house, we both kneeled by bedsides and poured our hearts out.

- What is the plan?
- Help me to see it … to feel it.
- Let me be patient.
- Help me to love.

I experienced a similar pattern a couple of years earlier when two discs in my neck ruptured and grabbed onto my nerve. I experienced intense nerve pain in my neck, across my shoulder and down to my elbow finally fading into a numb, tingling sensation in my fingers. The pain consumed me. Ordinary things like soccer games were simply attended. I couldn't even focus on the game. Sitting through three hours of church was terribly difficult. I tried to distract myself with the chores and the driving of the kids to events, but the nerve was a red-hot poker and screamed for my attention.

Prayers were panicked. "Make it stop! Please take this pain away!" My demanding prayers were seemingly unanswered. I endured the pain for months. Eventually I sought help from an orthopedic surgeon who prescribed pain killers. I spent months living in a medicated fog taking just the right amount to slightly dull the pain, yet still function as a mom. My emotions were raw – always on the verge of exploding. My oldest daughter Aubreigh called me one day to ask about my neck and the results of the medication. She was in nursing school at Brigham Young University and was rightly concerned about me. I burst into tears. "I can't do this any longer. This isn't fair. I don't think I can live with pain for the next 50 years." I sobbed. I felt beaten. She was patient with me. Her medical opinions and calm voice reached in through the cellphone and gave me a glimmer of hope. It was a turning point for me.

My prayers changed. "Heavenly Father help me to endure this well. What am I to learn from this?" I already knew. My heart and soul now wept for those who have trials involving chronic pain. Experience for me led to understanding and empathy. Chronic pain consumes your energy. It tests you physically, emotionally and spiritually. We've all heard the stories of good people hooked on pain killers. I'm so sorry to have ever judged them. We are all on difficult paths at times which zap our strength. Who am I to judge another? I apologized to God for previous judgments.

Eventually I found a pain doctor who was able to greatly reduce the inflammation in my neck with a series of injections. Finding him was no accident. The doctor was mentioned to my husband by someone who knew of my condition. Looking back the timing was critical. The lessons weren't yet learned. When my heart was humbled and teachable, I found some relief. Thoughts and opinions and emotions toward others with trials involving sickness and pain had changed. The two-way communication had been opened and my relationship with Heavenly Father was given another chance to grow a little bit stronger. This was a tough hike. Lessons learned are real. My soul was changed.

Pray More Often Than You Brush Your Teeth

President Gordon B. Hinckley taught us often about prayer. *"Brethren and sisters, I know that you are a praying people. That is a wonderful thing in this day and time when the practice of prayer has slipped from many lives."* [7] We are taught as Primary children to say our prayers every morning and every night. A righteous pattern started early on. The scriptures are clear on communicating with the Lord in this pattern:

"Counsel with the Lord in all thy doings, and he will direct thee for good; yea, when thou liest down at night lie down unto the Lord, that he may watch over you in your sleep; and when thou risest in the morning let thy heart be full of thanks unto God; and if ye do these things, ye shall be lifted up at the last day" (Alma 37:37).

Elder David A. Bednar talked about our morning and evening

prayers in the October 2008 general conference. He said if our morning prayers are looking out toward the day and what's coming, then we are previewing the day in our prayer. Our evening prayers are a reporting to the Lord on what has happened through the course of the day. We may be thanking Him for blessings received, reviewing our thoughts and concerns, and repenting of a few things that happened that were not right.[8]

It is a healthy pattern. So is brushing your teeth twice a day. Good practice. Good for you. When I taught seminary I used to tell my students that if they weren't praying more often than they brushed their teeth, they could do better. That's because there is a deeper relationship in counseling with the Lord throughout the day.

"Cry unto God for all thy support; yea, let all thy doings be unto the Lord, and whithersoever thou goest let it be in the Lord; yea let all thy thoughts be directed unto the Lord; yea, let the affections of thy heart be placed upon the Lord forever" (Alma 37:36).

Sometimes the prayer is simple in times of stress and crisis – "Help!" Other times it is like communicating our thoughts in an ongoing fashion. These prayers can be brief throughout the course of the day. It begins to flow out of us naturally if practiced. The closer we get to Him, the more this ongoing communication happens automatically.[9]

When life gets tough and the trail is stressful it really helps me to pray throughout the day. It helps me because my thoughts can quickly spiral into a negative cycle. Worries about one of my kids or health or marriage issues or 100 other worries can quickly turn into the what-ifs. When I catch myself going there, I can immediately offer a prayer asking for help in stopping the negative cycle and for help in turning my fear over to faith. I can say, "I recognize I'm doing this and I'm trying to take a higher road. Please help me as I try harder." It makes sense to me to communicate throughout the day and then in the evening to discuss the day's events and take a spiritual inventory of sorts.

The result is a closer and deeper relationship. A friendship. It's similar to spending the day talking with a really good friend. I like to think of Heavenly Father as my friend. It helps influence the frequency of my prayers and the feeling that I want to communicate everything to Him. I want to turn and talk to Him about what's going on at the moment. There are many times in the scriptures where the Lord refers to us as "a friend." One of my favorites: *"Verily I say unto you my friends, fear not, let your hearts be comforted ... "* (D&C 98:1).

Find Your Channel

It was a frantic search. My young children scurrying everywhere. It was a massive hunt to find the most important item in our household that had been misplaced. Dad was not happy. The TV remote control was gone. Where could it be? I've heard it said that when Mom is not happy, the whole house is not happy. I can trump that. When Dad's remote is missing – not a good day. And so it was a united effort. All of us circling around each other looking under every piece of furniture, in toy boxes and in drawers. In a busy household with four young children, it could have been anywhere.

As we continued to search with no success, our moods sunk and Dad's anger rose. We repeated our search – looking again in the same locations. I hadn't noticed that my little daughter Amber had left the area. Just as I had about given up, Amber walked out. She walked over to the couch, lifted up a cushion and pulled out the remote. "Here it is," she said with a big grin.

We couldn't believe our eyes. We had searched that couch multiple times. We were in disbelief. "How did you do that?" we asked. I've never forgotten what she said. "I just went back to my bedroom and said a prayer that Heavenly Father would help me find the remote for Dad and He told me where to look." Amber knew at a very young age that prayers were not something we do only at church. She already understood the principle Alma taught in the Book of Mormon when he said, *"Do ye suppose that ye cannot worship God save it be in your synagogues only?"* (Alma 32:10)

"Houses of worship have their place. However, with the exception of the temple, they are not typically the place where we learn the greatest spiritual lessons. It is on our knees, in our homes and closets, where the greatest worship takes place. It is also here where the greatest spiritual experiences are received. Prophets over the ages have rarely received their major revelations in chapels or synagogues."[10] Amber learned an important lesson that day – a lifetime lesson. That day she learned that her Heavenly Father was always ready to listen. Whenever and wherever.

Imagine if we had to bottle up all of our prayers only to release them on Sundays in the chapel. I often thank Heavenly Father for the principle and gift of prayer. What a beautiful gift – direct communication straight to the source. With all the distractions in our lives it is so important to find a place where we can be honest with Him. A channel that directly tunes into Him. "God has provided a channel of communication between Him and his children on earth that Satan, our common enemy, cannot invade. This is the channel of secret prayer. The significance of this to the Latter-day Saint is profound, for by this means we are able to communicate with our Heavenly Father in secrecy, confident that the adversary cannot intrude."[11] How important that we find our channel.

I love Amulek's words in the Book of Mormon when he teaches us how and where to pray:

"But this is not all; ye must pour out your souls in your closets, and your secret places, and in your wilderness" (Alma 34:26).

Note the descriptive words. In other verses he has suggested crying unto God in many different circumstances. In this verse he does not use the phrase "cry unto him." Instead his words suggest something more must take place in our closets. This is where true, pure emotion and energy is expended. The image is that we "pour out our souls" like water out of a pitcher. The pitcher is emptied after the pouring. This signifies that nothing is held back or hidden. We have been completely honest and forthright with the Lord and ourselves. It is the time of greatest spiritual vulnerability and honesty when our will has been submitted to Heavenly Father's will. As in all things, the greatest example comes from the Savior, who alone in the Garden of Gethsemane, poured out his soul unto death.[12] Certainly the Savior had found His channel.

Your channel of secret prayer can take place in a variety of places in your own wilderness. Years ago when I was suffering from depression, I had to drive 45 minutes into downtown Phoenix for work. Mornings were always the most difficult. My channel everyday was in my car. I poured my soul out to Heavenly Father each morning on the road pleading for help that my emotions might make it through yet another day. As a young mother raising four children, there were days that my patience and energy was truly tested. I remember stealing just a few minutes on hard days in my closet. It was a place that I could remove myself for just a few minutes…sometimes seconds…to look to my Heavenly Father for added energy to make it to the kids' bedtime. Sometimes my channel was my closet.

In my later years I've developed a love for nature and the outdoors. The Arizona sunshine and the desert air feed my soul. I feel the same energy when I hike the beautiful mountains of Park City, Utah, in the summer. My channel is clear and direct and open when I walk or hike. My legs and lungs are busy and working, yet my mind is clear from distractions and open to receive. This new channel in my life has been the greatest blessing in strengthening my relationship with Him.

Sometimes conditions are such that words cannot be verbally expressed to our Heavenly Father. This channel is silent but no less powerful. Heart and soul express deep emotion that is received and embraced by our

Heavenly Father. We are heard just the same.

A tender section of the Book of Mormon is found in Mosiah 24 and tells of the children of God who cried out because their afflictions were so great. Amulon put guards over them to watch. Anyone found calling upon God to help them would be put to death. We learn from the writings that the people didn't raise their voices to God. Instead they silently poured out their hearts and He knew the thoughts of their hearts:

"And it came to pass that the voice of the Lord came to them in their afflictions, saying: Lift up your heads and be of good comfort, for I know of the covenant which ye have made unto me; and I will covenant with my people and deliver them out of bondage" (Mosiah 24:13).

The next verse is particularly tender and precious to all of us who have felt forgotten or destitute or hopeless at the thought of ever over-coming our burdens. This promise applied to this group of people under terrible conditions is absolutely a promise to us today:

"And I will also ease the burdens which are put upon your shoulders, that even you cannot feel them upon your backs, even while you are in bond-age; and this will I do that ye may stand as witnesses for me hereafter, and that ye may know of a surety that I, the Lord God, do visit my people in their afflictions. And ... the Lord did strengthen them that they could bear up their burdens with ease, and they did submit cheerfully and with patience to all the will of the Lord" (Mosiah 24:14-15).

Note that the Lord doesn't immediately remove their burden, but He does lighten their load. It must have been comfort of a spiritual and emotional nature that spoke to their hearts. He strengthened and support-ed them. The first time I really read this story with an experienced under-standing of trials, I wept. I wept for the despair they must have felt. I wept as I read the principle taught and now understood this form of communi-cation. He not only receives those heart messages, but His voice can come to me in my afflictions. It is a voice of deliverance. It is a voice of hope. It is a voice of peace. And it can travel in a channel directly from my heart to His.

Find your channel. A few years ago I had to find one at the bottom of the ocean. A desperate prayer. No words able to be spoken – just my heart to His – at the bottom of the ocean.

It was a fabulous dive trip. My husband, Kevin, and I traveled to the other side of the world with a group of friends. Destination: Micronesia. We went to dive World War II wrecks which were sunk in battle and now lay on the bottom of the ocean. I was nervous about the adventure, but I had over 100 dives under my belt and felt capable and experienced enough.

One particular dive during the middle of the week is seared forever in my memory. We had a guide willing to take us down deep into the belly of a ship into the engine room. Only the more experienced were invited. My husband and I and about six others eagerly signed up. Just before sunset we jumped from the dive boat into the water below. We dropped down to the surface of the boat at about 80 feet. Through a small opening we entered the lower level of the ship. Down we went through tight dark hallways. Deeper and darker. We each carried our own flashlights which illuminated only the immediate area in front of us. We had turned and twisted so many times that I had no idea where I was. I wondered if Kevin knew. He looked back once and flashed the hand signal for, "are you okay?" I checked my computer to see how much air I had left at this depth. All good. I flashed the okay sign back at him.

More rooms. The kitchen. Sleeping quarters. It was fascinating and somber to tour this sunken graveyard. I began to wonder how much longer. I was checking my computer more often now. Then we took a turn. This was the final plunge deep down to the engine room. Each of us slowly and carefully moved our bodies in a head down position as we swam down a long spiral staircase toward the final destination. Eight bodies in a line and upside down in very close quarters.

And then the lights dimmed and everything stopped. Our guide's flashlight had died. He was in complete darkness and couldn't see to lead us. He pulled out his backup flashlight from a pocket. Dead. In addition, the front diver's regulator hose had twisted around a piece of metal. She was stuck. Those of us in the back and the middle of the group couldn't see what was happening. All we knew is that we were hanging upside down in the dark for a very long time. If any one of us panicked it could be disastrous for all of us. I checked my computer. Ten minutes of air left at this depth.

I found my channel. My heart to His. "Heavenly Father please help me to stay calm. Please help all of us to stay calm. Help ... " Immediately the thought came. Cut your breathing down in half. I concentrated on breathing at half the normal rate to conserve what little air I had left. I hoped that Kevin was doing the same. It was so tight that I couldn't even turn to look at him. But the panic never came. I was at peace. I was not alone. Upside down in the bottom of a ship at the bottom of the ocean I knew that Heavenly Father knew exactly where I was. My secret place. My wilderness.

Eventually another diver up front had been able to get a backup flashlight to the dive master who was leading. The front diver's hose was freed. What was several minutes had felt like hours and finally we could move forward. "Thank you, Heavenly Father." Prayers of gratitude flew up my channel as we found our way out of the shipwreck and back to the dive boat in safety.

What a gift. We are not alone. The significance of this channel of secret prayer? Essential. Crucial. Life-saving.

Recognizing a Response

My daughter Amber, had just returned home from church. The lesson in the Young Women meeting had been about finding your gifts. She was still a young teenager at the time and wondered if she had a gift. She decided to make it a matter of prayer. "Please help me to know my gift."

The next afternoon her friend called her unexpectedly. "Amber," the friend said. "you know what is special about you? You will go out of your way to make people happy. If you like something, but someone else doesn't, then you will just stop and do what makes the other person happy so they won't be sad or mad. I just thought of that and wanted to call and tell you."

Amber hung up the phone and knew that it was an answer to her prayer. Her heart and mind were open to receiving and recognizing the response. This answer happened to come from a conversation with a friend. Answers can come in so many different forms. I have received answers in scripture, in song, in gospel doctrine class, in Relief Society lessons, in radio conversations while driving, in emails, in service – the list is endless. Too often we pray and then jump up and move on to the many duties of the day without consciously looking for that response. It's going about our day while trusting in our heart that the Lord will provide in His time. When we fully commit to the Lord in a two-way conversation, we are committing our voice in prayer and we then commit to listen for His. Listening is more than not talking – it is recognizing a response.[13]

Gordon B. Hinckley said, *"Be prayerful. You can't do it alone. You know that. You cannot make it alone and do your best. You need the help of the Lord … and the marvelous thing is that you have the opportunity to pray, with the expectation that your prayers will be heard and answered. … He stands ready to help. Don't ever forget it."*[14]

Austin had moved up to the Provo area to attend Utah Valley University. It was a healthy change of scenery. He was moving forward with his life. We all felt like it was the right thing to do. I was proud of him for courageously moving into an apartment with unknown roommates. He was unpacked, settled in and registered for his classes. There would no doubt be questions about the mission. He and I spoke about the best way to answer those. "Be honest," I said. "You did your best. I'm proud of you. Shoulders back. Head up. Be proud of yourself and your service."

The only thing left – Austin needed a job. On this new leg of life he needed to be self-sufficient. He filled out dozens of applications online. Nothing. I made it a matter of prayer. For weeks I asked Heavenly Father to bless Austin that he would be able to find a job that could support him financially and emotionally. I also asked that I might somehow be instrumental in helping him find something – even though I was 800 miles away.

I was walking through the desert on my way back home from a 3-mile power walk. Almost home. A large drink of water was sounding good about now. And then came the answer. A strong thought – a thought that came suddenly with urgency. Go home…get on the church website… look at jobs in Provo. I didn't understand it, but I recognized it and so I acted. After eventually pulling up the job listing in the Provo area I saw it. "Open position: Cashier in the Provo temple. Part time." My heart swelled. I called Austin. He applied immediately.

The next day came the phone call. "Mom – I got the temple job." We cheered together on the phone. What better place for this young man to work and emotionally heal than the temple. I hung up and fell to my knees. Tears of gratitude flowed. What a tender mercy. Heavenly Father had heard and responded to a mother's heart.

"Draw near unto me and I will draw near unto you; seek me diligently and ye shall find me; ask, and ye shall receive; knock, and it shall be opened unto you" (D&C 88:63).

Seek me diligently. What does that word mean? The dictionary defines it as constant in an effort to accomplish something.[15] It means more than the time you spend on your knees asking. It means being specific about asking for something and anticipating a response. Is our request specific enough? If the request is broad and general, Heavenly Father may not be able to show us an answer that we would recognize or attribute to the prayer. To be constant in an effort, to accomplish something would entail carrying that mental thought with us throughout the days, week, months or years, requires vigilance.

Remember that we have learned that there are blessings out there that God is willing to grant. We just need to ask. A specific prayer received and granted with an immediate response is a mercy. A beautiful blessing which immediately bridges the gap between us and God. It is clear and powerful and builds our testimony.

My young nephew, Nick, was scheduled for a complicated eye surgery which would allow his non-working eye to focus. My parents contacted everyone in the entire extended family for a family fast the day before the surgery. We all were to pray for Nick's recovery and also for the surgeon. We prayed that the doctor's hands would be steady and that his mind would be sharp and know exactly what to do. Nick's parents waited anxiously in the waiting room at the hospital. When the surgeon came out of surgery and walked into the waiting room, he was crying. He asked if there were prayers in his behalf. "Yes," they explained. "The entire family had fasted and prayed." The surgeon was very choked up and explained that he felt his hands guided during the entire operation. He said that he knew that God was in charge of that surgery. An experience never forgotten by a surgeon. An answer to a family prayer never forgotten by those who love Nick. Testimonies strengthened.

Sometimes answers come in unexpected packages. A mercy that must be seen with spiritual eyes looking for and recognizing it.

I pulled out of my driveway early one morning in October headed for Utah. My daughter Amber, was delivering her first baby boy. If I planned it right I would arrive at the hospital just in time to help her through the labor pains. My older daughter Aubreigh was close by and we were all eager for this new arrival.

I was about three hours south of the Provo, Utah, area when my cellphone rang. It was Aubreigh. "Mom – Amber is pushing." It was unlikely that I would make the birth. It's all good. My older daughter was there at the hospital with Amber's husband, Sean, to help. The next phone call about an hour later was from Amber. "Mom – he's not breathing. The doctors are working on him. He came out blue. Everybody's in the corner working on him. Sean had consecrated oil for the blessing of the sick in his pocket. They gave him a blessing then took him away. Hurry ... "

My foot punched the gas pedal. I began driving much too fast. The what-ifs flooded my mind. Fear of the unknown. What if Amber lost this baby? How would she ever recover? I tried to concentrate on the road, but driving safely was secondary to anguish. Gut-wrenching anguish.

I recognized the fear and knew I needed to turn it over. What good would I be to my daughter if I rolled my car in an accident? I lowered my speed and began to pray. "Heavenly Father, please bless this little family. If it be Thy will that this baby boy live, then please bless the doctors and nurses to know how to help him. Please give Amber peace. Calm my soul. Please bless my faith ... " Requests were rattled off with raw emotion.

A short time later, I was driving up Interstate-15 about an hour south of the hospital. I had surrendered my mind and heart to the Lord. He was in control. I put it all in His hands. Soon I would arrive at the hospital and face the situation. There were dark clouds all around. It had been raining on and off during the drive up. Then it happened. The clouds parted for just a moment and the sun came through. Beautiful colors filled the clouds. The sun strained to shine through the mist. It was majestic. And it was for me. A tender mercy. A recognized response to a desperate prayer.

As I walked into the hospital delivery room my oldest daughter Aubreigh met me. "It's going to be okay, Mom. He scared us but Amber and baby are okay." She was surprised at my calmness. "Yes, I know," I whispered.

Faith in His Timing

What about those heartfelt, gut-wrenching, pleading prayers that seem unanswered? Prayers where we really feel that we know best. Why aren't they answered? Where is the relief? Are you really there, God?

It hit me like a ton of bricks. A slap in the face. I had prayed nearly 24 hours straight since receiving the first phone call from the MTC. A decision would be made tomorrow regarding Austin coming home or not. I prayed with heart and soul that he would stay – that he would get on that plane to Russia. I pushed every ounce of faith in me toward that miracle. I was bold in my prayers and felt my faith could make it happen.

The call. "Come pick up your son." A slug in the stomach. A jolt to my faith. A blatantly unanswered prayer. It shook me to the core.

Earlier we learned about seeking Him diligently and we would receive, and doors would be opened (D&C 88:63). The principle that immediately follows in the next verse is critical to our understanding:

"Whatsoever ye ask the Father in my name it shall be given unto you, that is expedient for you" (D&C 88:64).

Notice that it is not just – it shall be given unto you. That word – expedient. The Father will decide the WHEN and the WHERE and even the IF in the giving. We ought to remember that we don't dictate to God the timing of His answers to us and the content of what comes in response to our prayers. We don't tell Him what and when. That only comes according to His will and His timing and His wisdom. It's knowing that He loves us. It's trusting that He knows what is best for us. Our job is to be open. Willing and ready to receive.[16] For as long as it takes. Somewhere in the trial there is something to be learned. The lesson isn't over yet. Maybe it's a lesson for you. Maybe it's a lesson for someone else within the scope of the trial. It is the ultimate test of trust. It is living by faith. It takes work. And yes – it is hard.

The words in the song "Unanswered Yet" describe it well.

Unanswered yet? The prayer your lips have pleaded
In agony of heart these many years?
Does faith begin to fail, is hope departing,
And think you all in vain those falling tears?
Say not the Father hath not heard your prayer;
You shall have your desire, sometime, somewhere.

Unanswered yet? Nay, do not say ungranted;
Perhaps your part is not yet wholly done;
The work began when first your prayer was uttered,
And God will finish what He has begun.
If you will keep the spirit burning there,
His glory you shall see, sometime, somewhere.[17]

There are many who suffer. For many of us the trail seems too steep to bear. At times we teeter on the edge. The hike is too difficult. And we feel all alone. During the darkest of times I must only cling to two truths. God knows me and God loves me. If I really believe that – know that – then I can wake up the next day and try again.

Seemingly unanswered prayers. My legs burned and my lungs worked overtime as they pulled me up the mountain. I uttered the same request in prayer that I had done so for many months. "Please help me find my path. What is my purpose?" The last of my four children had left home for college. They were all in Utah now and my husband and I were living in Arizona. I was officially an empty-nester.

I spruced up my resume and wrote cover letters. Every day I spent hours on the computer applying for jobs. Teaching seminary for four years had given me teaching experience and my bookkeeping experience for my husband's firm was ongoing. My prayers continued. The high school called and wanted interviews for a variety of positions. "This must be it," I thought. Heavenly Father wants me to stay involved with youth. Interviews were positive, but offers couldn't materialize because of one small thing or another. I called other firms about part-time bookkeeping opportunities. "Nothing right now. We'll call you in the future." I felt like I was at a dead end. Seemingly unanswered prayers.

And then came a thought. This wasn't what I was supposed to do. God had a plan for me. I just needed to find it. I couldn't see it – I wasn't ready to see it. Heavenly Father was nudging me toward it. Patience.

I poured myself into service. Meals for the sick. Brownies for the ward party. Cannery assignments. Missionary work. I poured energy into the scriptures. Institute every week. Studied for gospel doctrine lessons. Desperate to find answers anywhere – somewhere. A need to recognize hope.

Faith in God includes faith in His timing. I never lost my faith in God as I talked to Him every single day about the same thing. He never lost faith in me. Prayers changed as I discussed my specific needs. No more generalities. "Please Heavenly Father – help me to see it. Let me feel it. Bless that my spirit will recognize."

Eventually subtle thoughts began to creep back in. Those thoughts about writing a book that I'd had over the past couple of years. Thoughts that I hadn't been ready to receive. Thoughts that I'd pushed back into a dusty corner of my mind and refused to recognize. Really? Write a book?

Suddenly it felt real. It felt true.

And so I write. The words flow so fast I can hardly keep up. Clearly the path that I am supposed to take for now. An unanswered prayer? Yes and no. Yes – unanswered in my time frame. Unanswered in the way that I expected. But answered in His timing. I had to do the work. The process required to get to the answer was necessary training for me. A lesson. A gift from Him.

Praise the Mount

Be grateful. We've all heard it. Counsel given by professionals in the world of psychology. Counsel given by our prophet. Counsel in the scriptures. Easy to remember on those easy hikes of life strolling through the wildflower. Not so easy on moderate and difficult life hikes when it feels more natural to throw a pity party instead.

During really difficult times I have adopted this commandment of gratitude. There are times that prayers have become so repetitive with requested blessings and rescue that I feel redundant. It quickly becomes a cycle in which I am at the core and life is spinning out of control around me. Gratitude takes the spotlight off me and turns it outward. I call them my gratitude prayers. There have been many long days and hikes where only gratitude prayers were expressed. I tell Heavenly Father that I'm not going to ask for anything. I know He already knows my heart. For days I can go through lists of things I'm grateful for. A warm blanket. A pillow under my head. A hot shower. Healthy legs that can carry me up the mountain. I get right down to the basics. Something in my soul lifts when I practice this.

Psychologists have long stated that it is impossible to be grateful and experience stress at the same time. Robert A. Emmons, a researcher at the University of California Davis conducted extensive research on gratitude. He and his colleagues asked participants to keep daily or weekly gratitude journals. Those who kept gratitude journals:

- Exercised more regularly and reported fewer physical symptoms. They felt better about their lives as a whole and were more optimistic about the upcoming week.
- Were more likely to progress toward personal goals.
- Reported higher positive levels of alertness, enthusiasm, determination, attentiveness and energy.[18]

Not only does the research encourage us to be grateful, but we have been commanded to do so. The prophet Alma said:

"And now I would that ye should be humble, and be submissive and gentle; easy to be entreated; full of patience and long suffering; being temperate in all things; being diligent in keeping the commandments of God at all times; asking for whatsoever things ye stand in need, both spiritual and temporal; always returning thanks unto God for whatsoever things ye do receive" (Alma 7:23).

This scripture suggests what kind of a person I ought to be, and unlike many that merely say, "keep the commandments," it points rather directly at the very nature of us. It says that we should return our thanks to God.[19] Note that the underlying tone of the scripture suggests hard times – not just good times. When we see words like patience and long suffering we are safe to assume that giving thanks is required regardless of which hike we're on. The blessing of gratitude is not only a way to show appreciation and love for our Heavenly Father, but an added measure of our own lifted spirit and contentment. For a moment we are commanded to be happy simply with what is.

The people of Alma were a great example of gratitude. We learned in Mosiah 24 of the Lord strengthening them and easing the burden on their backs. They demonstrated their nobility by remembering who had eased their burdens.

"And they gave thanks to God, yea, all their men and all their women

and all their children that could speak lifted their voices in the praises of their God" (Mosiah 24:22).

It is easy to have a grateful heart after the burdens have been lifted or eased. But it is so important to also possess a grateful heart during the burden.

Austin had been home from the MTC about three months when he came to me and said, "Mom I want to sing." He had sung quite a bit in the MTC and had learned some hymns in Russian. "I want to sing 'Come Thou Fount' in church. Will you accompany me?" We worked on the arrangement together. He wanted to sing some in English and some in Russian. He performed it beautifully. It was stirring. Many eyes were filled with tears.

Come, thou Fount of every blessing
Tune my heart to sing thy grace;
Streams of mercy, never ceasing,
Call for songs of loudest praise.
Teach me some melodious sonnet,
Sung by flaming tongues above.
Praise the mount! I'm fixed upon it,
Mount of thy redeeming love.

O to grace how great a debtor
Daily I'm constrained to be!
Let thy goodness, like a fetter,
Bind my wandering heart to thee.
Prone to wander, Lord, I feel it,
Prone to leave the God I love;
Here's my heart, O take and seal it,
Seal it for thy courts above.

During his burden, Austin still had a grateful heart. Grateful for his testimony. Grateful for the Atonement. Grateful to sing about it.

Communication with our Heavenly Father is the cornerstone of our relationship with Him. It takes practice. All relationships do. Isn't our relationship with Heavenly Father worth a bit more effort? Jesus Christ set the ultimate example. He was here to do His Father's will. Let us pour our heart and soul into this essential principle of prayer. It is finding your channel and then looking and listening for the response. Reach out and convey the desires of your heart. He will let you see His will for you. It is a process of faith and patience in His timing. Seek Him diligently. A key to finding hope.

Chapter 3

His Hands. His Voice. His Hug.

It was an ordinary paper route: 4:00 a.m. every morning. Lots of newspapers to deliver. My dad – then 14-year-old Clark – would walk or ride his bike delivering newspapers to his assigned territory. Those receiving his deliveries were both the young and old. Families all up and down the streets. And then there was that "old folk's home." Best to deliver and then get out of there. Clark was a little scared of old people.

It was Christmastime. Clark's dad knew the route. He knew there was an old woman at that "old folk's home" who was a customer. "Clark, you need to go see her and wish her a Merry Christmas." Clark didn't want to go. He knew it would be an uncomfortable situation. His wise father said, "I'll drive you." Clark's father rarely drove anywhere, except in necessary circumstances. Gasoline was expensive. Budgets were tight. Clark knew he meant business if he was willing to drive him to the home.

Along the way they stopped and bought flowers. The December air was cold and crisp. A winter wonderland. His dad waited in the car and sent Clark in.

"Hi. I'm your paper boy. I came to wish you a Merry Christmas."

She started to cry. With tears running down her cheeks she looked up at Clark and said, "You are the only person that has come to see me in a very long time."

A week later the phone rang at the house. It was the old folk's home. The old woman had died. Newspaper services would no longer be required. What a lesson. Even at the young age of 14, it shaped my father. It made an impact, and it changed his heart.

In the New Testament we read of a lawyer who asks Jesus which of the commandments is greatest:

"Jesus said unto him, Thou shalt love the Lord thy God with all thy heart, and with all thy soul, and with all thy mind. This is the first and great commandment. And the second is like unto it, Thou shalt love thy neighbor as thyself" (Matthew 22:37-39).

What a marvelous calling. An opportunity to bless and be blessed. A calling which allows us to serve the needs of others and at the same time lighten our own burdens. It is an attitude which softens our hearts and opens our minds to becoming more Christlike. It is following the perfect example that He set while on this Earth.

In Alma chapter 18 we read about the promises that we make at baptism. Promises that are so important that we need to be reminded of them often.

"And it came to pass that he said unto them: Behold, here are the waters of Mormon (for thus were they called) and now, as ye are desirous to come into the fold of God, and to be called his people, and are willing to bear one another's burdens, that they may be light;

"Yea, and are willing to mourn with those that mourn; yea, and comfort those that stand in need of comfort, and to stand as witnesses of God at all times and in all things, and in all places that ye may be in, even until death, that ye may be redeemed of God, and be numbered with those of the first resurrection, that ye may have eternal life" (Mosiah 18:8-9).

Let's look at those promises.

- Bear burdens that they may be light.
- Mourn with those that mourn.
- Comfort those that stand in need.
- Stand as a witness.

We committed ourselves. There are no contingencies stated. Only during good times? Only when it is convenient? Only if this particular life hike I'm on is easy? Regardless and whether or not life is easy or hard, these promises are required, are our duty and are a great commandment with great blessings attached.

A scripture in the Doctrine and Covenants begins to get to the heart, soul and mind of the matter:

"Wherefore, as ye are agents, ye are on the Lord's errand; and whatever ye do according to the will of the Lord is the Lord's business" (D&C 64:29).

You see how the relationship changes? We move from almost a requirement to loving the Lord by loving our neighbor. When we love others, we love the Lord. When we serve others, we serve the Lord. What a simply beautiful way to look at it. In lifting others, we are lifting ourselves.

Neal A. Maxwell said, *"It is abundantly clear, therefore, that we have a duty to comfort others, to mourn with them, to serve them, and to help them. When there is so much to do to help others, there is little time for self-pity. We do not know all the details of the crosses others bear, but we know enough to understand that crosses are being borne valiantly. Moreover, the courage of others can be contagious."*[1]

We serve because the Savior did. To serve is to become more like Him.

I'm In 'til It's Over

Nobody makes it back to live with Heavenly Father all by themselves. The Plan is not set up as a journey meant to be hiked as individuals all alone. We love and support each other as imperfect beings trying to do our best and trying to do His will. Our wards are set up in part as a means to fulfill this principle of service.

"The church is not a place where perfect people gather to say perfect things, or have perfect thoughts, or have perfect feelings. The church is a place

where imperfect people gather to provide encouragement, support, and service to each other as we press on in our journey to return to our Heavenly Father," [2] Elder Joseph B. Wirthlin said.

There is a word in African spirituality which describes the essence of a person's character. The word is Ubuntu and it means "I am because we are." A person with Ubuntu is open and available to others knowing that he or she belongs to a greater whole. Ubuntu speaks particularly about the fact that you cannot exist as a human being in isolation. It speaks about our interconnectedness. You cannot be human all by yourself and when you have this Ubuntu quality, you are known for your generosity. It is understanding that you are connected and what you do affects the whole world. When you do well, it spreads out. It is for the whole of humanity. [3]

I can think of no greater example of a group of imperfect people providing necessary, encouraging and loving service than the saints of the 8th Ward in Hyde Park, Utah. My dad, Clark Cederlof, continued on through his life with that changed heart from his experience as a 14-year-old boy at the old folk's home to a life filled with serving others. His spiritual eyes always catch sight of the underprivileged, the lonely, the misfit, the sick. He serves because the Savior did. And never did he imagine a time when tables would be turned and he would need to be the recipient of such service.

It was February of 2013. My dad was stricken with a serious case of shingles which affected the right side of his face, including his eye. He had 11 shingles inside his eyeball and two on the outside lens. The shingles on his skin ran across his eyebrow, forehead and nose. The University of Utah said that it was one of the worst cases they had seen. Because of the seriousness nobody could predict how long the pain would continue. The burning and shocking pain from the shingles on the optical nerves was excruciating – shooting rays of pain through his head every time he moved his eye. It affected his overall health and it quickly became clear that he would be unable to function on his little ranch. For years he had been raising beef cows and also had horses. Now he was confined to bed.

I traveled up to the Logan, Utah, area to visit Dad and encourage Mom who was his constant companion and nurse. Phone conversations with Mom had not prepared me for the sight of Dad. I'd never in my life seen him in such a state. The pain was in control and the strong cowboy that I was used to seeing was nowhere found in this reduced form. He couldn't open his eye. It was all we could do to get him out of bed to eat. I wondered how long this would last and how the ranch chores would be done.

Dad called his good friend, Richard, upon discovering how serious the disease was. Richard's immediate response – "no worry." The following Sunday, Richard assembled a group of Melchizedek Priesthood holders and informed them that Dad was going to need help caring for the live-stock and other ranch chores. He needed volunteers for the morning and afternoon feedings which would require about 30 minutes each. My dad's home teacher, Ken, stepped forward for the afternoon feed. Richard asked, "How many days can you serve?" Ken's response – "I'm in 'til it's over." Then the scoutmaster, Scott, who had worked with my dad in the Aaronic Priesthood said, "I'll take the morning feed and I'm in 'til it's over."

We had no idea the shingles would burn and torment and linger far beyond what doctors predicted. Several weeks later I returned for another visit. Late in the afternoon I caught sight of Dad's home teacher and his son throwing the hay bales. It was hard work. Surely there were other things in the home teacher's life that needed his attention. His son was a high school athlete. A teenager devoting a portion of every afternoon to my dad. Incredible. Inspiring.

I walked out and introduced myself. "How's your dad?" they asked.

"In bed," I said. "It's tough. I want to thank you both for this great service." I continued. "I know that nowhere in the home teaching manual does it require something like this." I choked back tears. "Thank you just isn't enough for what you are doing for my dad."

"We're here until he's better," they replied. It had been about eight weeks now.

Dad remembers hearing Scott's truck at 6:30 every morning as he stopped by on the way to work. It was the spring of the year and the corrals were muddy and conditions were difficult. But never a complaint. Dad's neighbor, Gary, a practicing physician, came over every Thursday on his day off to check on the hay supply. When needing to be replenished, he borrowed Dad's pickup truck and drove to the farmer who supplied some of the hay. The Aaronic Priesthood organized service projects on several occasions to prune back bushes and trees in preparation for summer. Sisters in the ward brought food and get-well cards and beautiful little paper flowers made by their children. My two brothers, Scott and Chad, traveled a distance to give Dad a blessing. Bishop Knudson and his counselors made multiple visits and blessed Dad with administrations.

On Sunday, even though most often confined to bed, Dad would put on clean jeans and a fresh clean shirt because the Aaronic Priesthood would be coming with the Sacrament. In a time when it was a struggle just to get through the week, Dad looked forward to this sacred time. When those boys administered the Sacrament it was a moment of hope. A time to remember the Savior. A time to hope for a better tomorrow.

On Easter Sunday in April, my dad was able to open his eye just enough to barely read the scriptural account of the Savior's sacrifice. It was the first time he had read anything since the shingles started. I called him on the phone. We talked about the meaning of Easter. I reminded him that in the Garden of Gethsemane the Savior felt the pain of shingles. The realization of that was humbling. We both wept.

At 12 weeks Dad was able to take over the ranch chores. He stayed in bed most of the time, but was determined to return to his chores. His ward had served him well. Dad's first opportunity to return to church was in September. He felt like he could endure the pain enough to get through Sacrament meeting. He wanted to bear his testimony and his heart and his soul to the members of the congregation. An entire ward changed from this experience. Certainly Dad was blessed by the service from the members of the ward, but I also know that as they served him, their hearts turned toward God. They all felt it. Testimonies strengthened. Hope realized. And there wasn't a dry eye in the meeting.

It has been over two years now. The shingles pain is still there. It is a bit better – some days better than others. Dad's heart is changed. Softer. More tender. He can't speak of the service rendered without tears. And so he goes forward. Continuing in his life of service. Looking for the underprivileged, the lonely, the misfit, the sick…

"And behold, I tell you these things that ye may learn wisdom; that ye may learn that when ye are in the service of your fellow beings ye are only in the service of your God" (Mosiah 2:17).

With his burden about him – he will continue to lift the burdens of others…

Crooked Hands

All of us have dark periods in our lives. What a blessing to receive kindness, encouragement and support during such dismal times. After we have reached the summit on the most difficult hikes, we encounter opportunities to pay that forward to others. We have the opportunity to be His hands – His voice – His hug. It speaks of our commitment to God and our level of conversion. To look and listen and seek ways to honor Him and serve others.

Elder Robert J. Whetten said, *"Every unselfish act of kindness and service increases your spirituality. God would use you to bless others. Your continued spiritual growth and eternal progress are very much wrapped up in your relationships—in how you treat others. Isn't the measure of the level of your conversion how you treat others?"*[4]

The people who make a difference in your life are not the ones with the most credentials, the most money, or the most awards. They are the ones that care. They are ordinary people with extraordinary hearts. They are ordinary people full of goodness.

What is goodness? Webster's dictionary defines goodness as *the state or quality of being good, specifically virtue, excellence, kindness, generosity and benevolence.*[5] I love the word benevolence. Benevolence is kindness…charity. Where have we heard the word benevolence? When we memorize the 13 Articles of Faith in Primary we read in the first part of the 13th Article of Faith:

We believe in being honest, true, chaste, benevolent, virtuous, and in doing good to all men …

In the book "Articles of Faith" by James Talmage, he adds that benevolence is founded on love for fellow men; it embraces, though it far exceeds charity, in the ordinary sense in which the latter word is used.[6] There are well-known people in history who magnify the definition of benevolent: Emma Smith, Mother Teresa and Mary – mother of Jesus.

I would like to introduce you to my definition of benevolent. Her name is Lucille Cederlof. She is my grandma. Because Cederlof is a big word for a little kid, she acquired the name of Grandma C for short. She lived a long 97 years of life. Ninety-seven years of selfless service to others. When I grow up, I want to be just like her.

Years ago, Grandma C was the mother of five small children. She was constantly in motion. Her children were taught that which was good and right and noble. Honesty was always an important lesson and the importance of helping others was taught frequently in the home. As an 11-year-old child herself, she received her patriarchal blessing from her grandfather. In that blessing one of the things she was told is that she would "grow to become a bright and shining light." How completely this has been fulfilled! She helped countless individuals with money, time, moral support or whatever was needed.

There was another family with five children on Grandma C's street who lost their mother to a brain tumor. Grandma C was up to the home nearly every day helping them get meals and a variety of other needs. I don't suppose anyone really knows exactly how much she did for them. At one of the boy's wedding some years later, Grandma C went through the reception line. When this boy saw her, he introduced her to his new bride by saying, "This is my other mother."

I remember Christmas Eve at her house one year. The phone rang and she received word of a little family that would have no Christmas presents. I remember the urgency as she grabbed her coat and rushed out the door to buy presents for that little family before the stores closed.

Grandma C rarely sat, but when she did it was productive. As she became frail physically, she crocheted blankets for the newborns and booties and little stocking caps to be sent abroad by church welfare services. Although her hands were tired and aching, they could still hug and love somebody. She knew that some baby, somewhere in the world, would know she loved them because she made them a blanket. Grandma C embraced hundreds. Each loving stitch represented her acceptance of those who were nearly forgotten. My dad was at her home for a visit and there was a time when she was just finishing a little stocking cap. She asked him if he liked the colors. He held the little cap and admired her handiwork. When he handed it back she was weeping. Weeping for babies born in poor circumstances.

She always told us, "I want you to tell me about anyone that needs financial help." If anyone in the family told a story of someone in a bind, she would walk over to her purse and pull out a check and start scribbling. It is important at this point to mention that Grandma C was neither rich nor poor, but chose to live in a thrifty manner. She could always find the means to help someone in need. I have heard her indicate her pleasure in buying toilet paper cheap at Albertsons to save a few pennies, but shortly thereafter I would learn that she had given someone in need $1,000.

Grandma C sought out those who were hurting and sorrowing. She had her own trials in life, but rather than stay home and lament her condition, she sought out others who were troubled. She served others every day of her life. For years she prepared food for those in her ward or neighborhood who had lost loved ones. She understood that it wasn't just the physical body that needed her nursing, but the soul. You nurse souls with love. Sometimes it was just a ring of the doorbell and a hello, or a phone call to check up on someone, or a quick hug on the street. Her love was endless.

I guess one could say that my Grandma C was a speckled pigeon. When her boys were young, her youngest son loved to raise pigeons and had quite a collection in cages behind the garage. There was one particular pigeon that was white and beautiful and loved to strut. One day the white pigeon laid an egg and proceeded to sit on the nest – most of the time. There was also a speckled pigeon which never laid any eggs, but would sit by the side of the nest next to the white pigeon. The white pigeon would often leave the nest to go strutting and leave the egg unattended. The speckled pigeon would quickly jump on the nest and look after the egg until the white pigeon returned. I think no further explanation is needed. Grandma C was a speckled pigeon.

Following the death of her husband, she served 19 years in an extraction assignment, which researches names for genealogical work. Originally she received a letter from the stake high council calling her to be an extraction worker. About the same time she was invited to be a worker in the Salt Lake Temple. She was torn as to which to do and so went to the Salt Lake Temple for guidance. During the temple session she prayed and asked if she should accept the calling in the extraction program. A voice exclaimed, "Of course you will." She wept when she would recall and tell us about that.

She went to the stake center three times a week – good weather and bad. She could read Old English. I used to call her when she was in her 80's to tell her I was coming for a visit to which she'd shout for joy and then say, "Now let me just check my calendar." At 80 years of age – checking her calendar! My dad asked her one day if the brethren had forgotten that she was continuing this extraction assignment after so many years. She replied, "I don't know, but the Lord hasn't."

There is one piece of her life that I have not mentioned. A physical trial that she battled nearly her whole life. As a young child I used to think that all grandmas had crooked hands – crooked hands and twisted bumpy fingers. It wasn't until I was a little older that I learned that she had rheumatoid arthritis. At its height, she was confined to bed all day long. There were years that the pain was so bad that she had to bathe and exercise her joints in hot mineral water every day. Yet she saw this as an opportunity to serve. She would gather up a group of other women with arthritis and take them out to the hot springs to soak. She never complained, but when we'd spend the night at her house, I would see her quietly reach for the big bottle of aspirin on the shelf before bedtime. Ultimately, all the knuckles of both hands had to be replaced through surgery. Crooked hands and painful joints throughout her body served everyone around her without complaint.

Ninety-seven years is a long time. Consider that those crooked hands prepared over 65,000 meals. Those crooked hands prayed 100,000 times and those crooked hands fell on the scriptures 30,000 times. When seeing herself in an old home movie or photograph of her younger years, she often would say, "Look at how pretty my hands used to be." I guess there are differences of opinion as to what constitutes pretty hands. When I think of all the good deeds and all the work those hands have done, there could be nothing more beautiful than her hands to me.[7]

Days before she passed away she requested that her hands be covered in the casket by a small white lace handkerchief. She didn't want them to be the focus. Throughout the viewing though, many of us peaked under that handkerchief. One last look at crooked hands – memories of love and service. Benevolent hands.

D&C 82:19 says that Zion is *"every man seeking the interest of his neighbor, and doing all things with an eye single to the glory of God."* Zion where are you? *"This promised Zion always seems to be a little beyond our reach. We need to understand that as much virtue can be gained in progressing toward Zion as in dwelling there. It is a process as well as a destination. We approach or withdraw from Zion through the manner in which we conduct our daily dealings, how we live within our families . . . how we seize opportunities to serve and do so diligently."*[8] The process of progressing toward Zion doesn't end when you graduate from high school. It doesn't end when you've completed a tough calling in the church. It doesn't end when the kids have grown and left the house. Progressing toward Zion may be a process that takes 97 years.

"Service changes people. It refines, purifies, gives a finer perspective and brings out the best in each one of us. It gets us looking outward instead of inward. It prompts us to consider others' needs ahead of our own. Righteous service is the expression of true charity, such as the Savior showed."[9] He was the perfect example. Now – does this mean that we must all be perfect? No. It doesn't mean that we don't make mistakes. It doesn't mean that we don't have frustrations and heartache in our lives. It just means that our hearts are right. That we are willing to try and try again – to protect our faith and to take time to love ourselves and others.

Perhaps our testimony of Him will be judged by the desires of our heart and also by the works of our hands. It is a commandment to serve others, yet the benefits and blessings are ours. *"As we extend our hands and hearts toward others in Christlike love, something wonderful happens to us. Our own spirits become healed, more refined and stronger. We become happier, more peaceful and more receptive to the whisperings of the Holy Spirit."*[10]

So let's ask ourselves – what will be our legacy? Most of us will never be famous on a worldly scale. But will we be that "ordinary" person with the extraordinary heart that makes a difference in someone's life? Whether young or old, we are building our own character – creating our own legacy – and teaching others along the way.

I look at my own hands. Long, straight fingers. Hoping they will work and love and serve as crooked once did.

A Missionary Promise

Life is full of challenges. We know from our understanding of the Plan that we voted for that. As we put one foot in front of another and plod through whatever circumstances surround us, wouldn't we eagerly sign up for anything which results in joy? We know from the scriptures, and some of us from experience, that there are few things in life that bring as much joy as assisting another in improving his or her life. We know that a full joy will come only through Jesus Christ, for *"in this world your joy is not full, but in me your joy is full"* (D&C 101:36). That joy is increased when efforts to help someone understand the teachings of the Savior decides to obey them, is converted, and joins His church.

"And if it so be that you should labor all your days ... and bring, save it be one soul unto me, how great shall be your joy ... " (D&C 18:15).

President McKay showed us how to obtain such joy with his profound clarification of our responsibility to share the gospel: "Every member a missionary." How seriously have we taken the Lord's charge to share His gospel? It is a lifelong responsibility.[11] Easier when trails are smooth – not foremost in our minds on rugged, steep trails. There is a huge need for each of us to open our mouths and share what we know and understand about happiness and about despair. Others notice the way that we live the gospel during difficult times. Though we may not feel or see our own light at times, it may be visible to somebody else who is ready for an increased understanding of this life – the good news that every child of God can again return to the Father who gave them life.

Why should we bear frequent and powerful testimony of Christ as our Savior and Redeemer? What could be better for us than hearing ourselves testify of the Atonement? Our spirit and testimony of the Atonement will carry us perhaps even more importantly than it will carry the investigators. When we struggle we know that Christ has our back. He is there beside us. We have reason to stand tall and be grateful that the Living Son of the Living God knows all about our sorrows and afflictions. As missionaries who wear a badge or as member missionaries who wear one on their heart the missionary promise is the same. It is a promise that if we are faithful in responding to a call to spread the gospel that He will bind up our broken hearts, dry our tears, and set us and our families free. Don't we all desire that?

The Savior said, *"Let your light so shine before men, that they may see your good works, and glorify your Father which is in heaven"* (Matthew 5:16). I don't know when the Lord will come again, but when He does – regardless of which hike I'm on – I want to be caught living the gospel. I want to be surprised right in the act of spreading the faith and doing good. I want the Savior to see the integrity of my heart and to know that despite difficult circumstances that I have, I've been trying to declare His word in the most compassionate way I could. Certainly He will know that I wasn't always successful, but that I honestly tried. It would be a true expression of my love for Him.[12]

Austin will forever be the greatest example to me of wearing the missionary badge on his heart despite enduring one of the most difficult periods of his life. As soon as he returned home to Arizona, he unpacked his missionary bags and supplies. While serving in the MTC he had acquired several Russian copies of the Book of Mormon. Though a long way from Russia he was determined to give them out. Though the missionary name tag was not hanging from his suit pocket, he would continue to seek out opportunities to share the gospel. He immediately placed a Russian Book of Mormon in the door panel of his truck.

Austin quickly found a job working as a cashier for a local restaurant. One day a woman was in line to purchase her food and was talking on her cellphone when she approached Austin. It only took him a moment to realize she was speaking in Russian. The woman lives in Moscow, Russia, and was visiting Arizona on business. Austin quickly initiated a conversation with her using his Russian language skills learned in the MTC. She asked how he knew the language and he explained the missionary program to her. The woman remembered a time many years prior when missionaries had visited her family in Moscow and told Austin that the two missionaries had told them about a man whose name she couldn't quite remember. Austin asked her if the name was Joseph Smith. "Yes!" she replied. Austin then took the opportunity to tell her in his new best Russian tongue about Joseph Smith and the First Vision. Everything in the restaurant seemed to fade away and no new customers approached as he continued to converse and bear testimony. The woman told Austin that she recognized the same feeling in her heart that she had felt so many years ago when two missionaries had shared their testimonies in her childhood home.

As the woman was seated for dinner, Austin ran out to his truck in the parking lot. He grabbed the Russian Book of Mormon and returned to the woman's table. "This is for you," he said. Together they read Moroni's promise. Austin bore his testimony of the power of prayer and wished her well.

Two months later Austin was busy working the same cash register when he heard someone speaking in Russian to him. He looked up and recognized the same woman who he had given the Russian Book of Mormon to. She was smiling. "I'm so happy to see you. I hoped you would be here." She told Austin that she had read the Book of Mormon and called the missionaries in Moscow to teach her. They were amazed that she had her own copy of the Book of Mormon in the Russian language and she told them about Austin. "I wanted to tell you that I am going to be baptized."

Austin came home that night and told me about the conversation.

"Mom, I have a baptism," he said with a smile.

"Yes, Elder Tucker, you do," I replied. Our hearts swelled. Indescribable joy.

A second Russian Book of Mormon was placed in the side pocket of the truck. Then a third. Then a fourth. Who knew that a cashier in Arizona could find Russian people to bear testimony to and continue to serve? The Lord knew.

Jeffrey R. Holland said it best: *"May we declare ourselves to be more fully disciples of the Lord Jesus Christ, not in word only and not only in the flush of comfortable times but in deed and in courage and in faith, including when the path is lonely and when our cross is difficult to bear."*[13]

It is easy to pull inward when in crisis. We want to shut the world out. But that is not where hope lies. We must reach outside ourselves. We must serve as He did. Both the giver and the receiver are blessed. As disciples of Christ, we are His hands. We are His voice. His hug. The act of serving in His name opens our heart and soul. We become soft. Open. Able to recognize hope.

Chapter 4

Words of Direction

I pull up to the base of Black Mountain ready to hike. When I look up at the mountain at the anticipated journey, there are two thoughts:
- I can do this.
- This is going to hurt.

I wonder if we had those same two thoughts before we came to Earth when we heard about the Plan. What we understood is that the Plan was set up for success. There were tools in place. When hiking a mountain we have access to tools as well. On a hot and sunny day there are things which will help us to successfully navigate and endure the journey: a bottle of water, good moisture-wicking socks, sturdy shoes and a cool breeze.

On our life hikes we battle difficulties, doubts and discouragements. We have talked about some of the tools which give us perspective and set us up for success. Prayer. Service. There is more.

In the New Testament, Paul was teaching and motivating the saints and trying to set them up for success:

"Take heed therefore unto yourselves, and to all the flock, over the which the Holy Ghost hath made you overseers, to feed the church of God, which he hath purchased with his own blood. For I know this, that after my departing shall grievous wolves enter in among you, not sparing the flock. Also of your own selves shall men arise, speaking perverse things, to draw away disciples after them" (Acts 20:28-30).

This is counsel from Paul testifying to the Saints – "Hey, it's tough out there and the wolves of the world are going to try to take your testimony." I love his words: "Take heed . . . to feed the church of God."

President Harold B. Lee said,

"There are those who have seemed to forget that the most powerful weapons the Lord has given us against all that is evil are His (the Lord's) declarations, the plain simple doctrines of salvation as found in the scriptures."[1]

How busy and distracted and stressed are we that this critical tool for success is ignored or pushed aside? We experience too much, suffer through the distresses of the world and see too much unhappiness to ignore His words of direction for us. It can be a direct line of communication for us. Personal and specific words applicable to our unique situation. Is this tool in your backpack? Is it sitting right next to your bed on the nightstand? All we need do is crack open the cover.

My mother is a living example of embracing the scriptures. In her later years of life she has continued to study and learn. Each semester she would sign up for another Institute class. How many times do you suppose she has read and re-read the Bible and the Book of Mormon? Too many to count. Yet, there she is up at the Utah State Institute once again reading, searching and pondering. It is a lifelong pursuit. An example not unnoticed by her children.

The scriptures have been referred to as living water. In the New Testament, the Savior refers to "living water" when he speaks to the woman drawing water at Jacob's well. He said,

"But whosoever drinketh of the water that I shall give him shall never thirst; but the water that I shall give him shall be in him a well of water springing up into everlasting life" (John 4:14).

The Savior's promise to this woman extends to each one of us. By going to the well daily and searching the scriptures, we will develop within ourselves a living spring that will quench eternally our thirst for happiness, peace and everlasting life.[2]

Elder Wirthlin continues: *"These latter days are a time of great spiritual thirst. Many in the world are searching, often intensely, for a source of refreshment that will quench their yearning for meaning and direction in their lives. They crave a cool, satisfying drink of insight and knowledge that will soothe their parched souls."*

Once I recognized my spiritual thirst for the scriptures and tasted of that source of refreshment in a meaningful way, I craved it. My testimony of the power found in the scriptures was solidified in teaching seminary. There is nothing like an incredibly difficult schedule of preparing five lessons each week to change your world. It is boot camp for the soul. I lived and breathed it and saw the majesty of the prophets' words in a new and exciting light.

Each morning as the students left the room, I would immediately sit down to prepare for the next day. One morning I looked at the schedule. We would be studying 2 Nephi 33 the following day. As usual, I prayed, then read, then studied, and studied some more – silently praying that the Spirit would lead me in a direction to teach what the students needed to hear. I read again from 2 Nephi 33:3-4:

"But I, Nephi, have written what I have written, and I esteem it as of great worth, and especially unto my people. For I pray continually for them by day, and mine eyes water my pillow by night, because of them ... and the words which I have written in weakness will be made strong unto them ... "

Posters of many of the Book of Mormon prophets lined the walls of my classroom. I looked up at them. What they must have sacrificed in writing the words for us! Nephi's emotions and pleading tugged at my heart. How his heart must have yearned for us to read and study the words. He knew the strength of them. And so I wiped my eyes and continued. Each semester was an attempt on my part to show my testimony and enthusiasm for the scriptures in hopes that my students would desire that for themselves.

Each summer was a welcome break from the hours of preparation and serious deficiency of required sleep. It was wonderful to break away from the nine months of routine and focus a bit on other things. But each summer it never took long to miss it and recognize a difference in my relationship with things of the Spirit. Toward the end of each summer I couldn't wait to get back to teaching seminary. I knew that the scriptures were clearly a conduit for which to receive that satisfying drink. The poster on the wall of my seminary room rang true to my heart:

If you want to talk to God ... pray
If you want God to talk to you ... read your scriptures.

We start early educating our children about the power found in scriptures. They recite scriptures each week in Primary. They sing about them in Primary songs. Have you really listened to the lyrics that their bright shiny faces sing in the favorite song called "Scripture Power"?

Because I want to be like the Savior, and I can,
I'm reading His instructions, I'm following His plan.
Because I want the power His word will give to me,
I'm changing how I live, I'm changing what I'll be.

I'll find the sword of truth in each scripture that I learn.
I'll take the shield of faith from these pages that I turn.
I'll wear each vital part of the armor of the Lord,
And fight my daily battles, and win a great reward.[3]

Hear His Voice

Is there any doubt that the scriptures – particularly the Book of Mormon – are meant for us? We learn in Mormon that Moroni is absolutely writing to us.

"Behold, I speak unto you as if ye were present, and yet ye are not. But

behold, Jesus Christ hath shown you unto me, and I know your doing" (Mormon 8:35).

The lessons and the teachings are for us. We know that with the Book of Mormon no other book has ever been written with such a full view of the future dispensation to which that record would eventually come.[4]

The first year that I taught seminary the study was New Testament. Oh how I loved and pondered the teachings! The second year was a study of the Book of Mormon. The third year – Doctrine and Covenants. What an inspiring surprise for me. I had never done justice to the pages. These sacred revelations are real – received in answer to prayer, in times of need, and came out of real-life situations involving real people.[5] That is why the study of the Doctrine and Covenants is so relevant to me and demands my attention.

When I taught D&C my third year of seminary, we spent some time on the "Explanatory Introduction" located just behind the title page. If you haven't taken the time to read it, I highly suggest that you do. There is an invitation to each of us. We read in the first paragraph that the Doctrine and Covenants is a collection of divine revelations and inspired declarations and that it contains an "invitation to all people everywhere to hear the voice of the Lord Jesus Christ, speaking to them … " In the third paragraph it beautifully states and reinforces that "in the revelations one hears the tender but firm voice of the Lord Jesus Christ … "

How encouraging and blessed are we to know this. As we study the lives of the early saints in both terrible and joyful times, we can see how they came to understand their situations. How they dealt with trials. It is easy to place ourselves in these pages and see and hear and feel the voice of the Lord direct our own individual paths. Different paths. Same voice.

It is a place where we can learn more about the Lord. It is a place where we can know him. A place where we can hear His voice.

Think of a time in your life when the Lord spoke to you personally – through scripture. Perhaps you were searching for an answer and you found it through study. Perhaps you had prayed and pondered for a time and then happened to open your scriptures and there it was. A tender mercy from the Lord.

My daughter Amber, came home from middle school one day with a solemn face. "How was your day?" I asked. Amber burst into tears. She proceeded to tell me that she had been with a group of friends at school who were using bad language. Amber wanted to be a part of the "cool" group and so she used a few swear words. It was clear that she felt bad about it. I gave her a hug and told her to go back to her room and have a talk with Heavenly Father about it. "Tell Him the story Amber. Then tell Him how you feel about it."

Amber did just that. And then she had a strong feeling to open up her scriptures. She picked them up and they fell open to D&C 25:3, *"Behold, thy sins are forgiven thee, and thou art an elect lady, whom I have called."* This is revelation to Emma Smith. But that day it was revelation to Amber.

She turned a few pages. *"Behold, verily, verily, I say unto you, that at this time your sins are forgiven you ... lift up your hearts and be glad"* (D&C 29:3-5) Once again the Lord's voice. Amber knew at that moment – the Lord knows me. He loves me.

Search, Ponder and Pray

Prophets throughout the scriptures and in the latter days have admonished us to search the scriptures, ponder them and pray for inspiration. Primary children sing melodies which reinforce that lesson.

In seminary I tried to instill in my students a desire to devour their scriptures. Every year the freshman would show up the first day with a brand new, shiny set of scriptures. The cover would creak when opened. Then I would show them mine. No more shine – the gold worn away. I flipped through the pages showing them passages highlighted, underlined and margins filled with comments and testimony and lessons learned. It is my spiritual journal. I kept pencils and pens readily accessible on the tables. "Mark it – journal it – circle it! When a scripture speaks to you – document your feelings about it." I hoped that they would catch the fever.

By the end of each year, the kids' scriptures were visibly worn. A beautiful sight. I had a freshman student one year show me his scriptures at the end of the year. "Look," he said, "my cover doesn't creak anymore." He was proud to own a "used" set of scriptures from our work that year.

One of our scripture masteries in seminary was 2 Nephi 32:3:

"… *feast upon the words of Christ; for behold, the words of Christ will tell you all things what ye should do.*"

The scriptures were not given to us for an occasional perusal or a casual reading. They were given so that we could "feast" on the words of Christ. This implies something much more than reading. To "feast" implies that the scriptures are satisfying a powerful spiritual hunger and quenching a thirst for the things of the Spirit. Those who enjoy this "feast" are those who hunger and thirst after righteousness. We are promised that we will be filled with the Holy Ghost as we feast upon the words of Christ in the scriptures. The spiritual food is internalized and becomes a part of us. Spiritually speaking you might say, "You are what you eat." The other verb that we see in the scriptures to describe our approach to scripture study is "to search."[6]

To search simply means to read – to find within the scriptures a direction for our own lives. It is to understand the revelations received by the prophets and to learn from the history of the people as they attempted to deal on the one hand with everyday life and on the other with the commandments. It was not always easy for them.

We read the Book of Mormon and say to ourselves, "How could they have been so foolish – they were successful when they lived the commandments and had nothing but problems when they didn't." Perhaps more important to consider were the feelings within the people as individuals when they had problems and were still keeping the commandments and following the prophets. A situation not unlike today.

I am intrigued by the use of the word "ponder." It says do more than read. In 3 Nephi 17:3 we read,

"Therefore, go ye unto your homes and ponder upon the things which I have said, and ask of the Father, in my name, that ye may understand, and prepare your minds for the morrow … "

Moroni 10:3 tells us that we must read the scriptures *"and ponder it in your hearts."* Ponder means to consider something deeply and thoroughly. To meditate or weigh carefully in the mind.[7] We must find meaning in the scriptures in our own lives. That is the ponder part. If we don't internalize them, then we are left with only knowledge, and although there is value in knowledge, it does not bring us salvation nor perfection.

In D&C 138, President Joseph F. Smith said,

"I sat in my room pondering over the scriptures … and reflecting … while I was thus engaged my mind reverted … and I was greatly impressed more than I had ever been" (D&C 138:1-6).

This is the process. Pondering the scriptures is a process – not an event. Searching and pondering gets us right within our heart and soul. We learn new applications for us as individuals and are reminded of the principles which apply to us and which we must apply to others. Prayer plays a role as we discuss with our Heavenly Father new insights and lessons which enlighten our mind. This process doesn't take place at one sitting. Rather it is a frame of mind which takes place over a period of time in which we are actively looking for the awakening. It is a process that opens the window to see and hear and feel the voice of the Lord, and to recognize His tender mercies.

Search, ponder and pray. These are the characteristics that make us teachable – that allow the spirit of our Heavenly Father to work within us. Without these principles in our lives, we run the risk of an intellectual commitment only, and that is very risky. It will not sustain us when we have to reach deep inside. When is that? During times of personal or family tragedy. During times of economic hardship. Or during times of serious personal temptation. These are the hard hikes.

Search, ponder and pray are also the basic elements in the perfection process. Without them there is no trail map. Some of us find our way by following others and there is good in that, but what if some of those we follow go in the wrong direction. We must chart our own course.[8]

Section 132 of the Doctrine and Covenants spoke to my heart and soul and inspired me to chart my own course when I was a teenager. I remember it like it was yesterday. I was given my first real set of scriptures. Leather bound with my name engraved on them. My mom and dad had given them to me when I was 17 years old – the year that I met my future husband.

I searched. Section 132 jumped off the page. Revelation given through Joseph Smith regarding eternal marriage. I highlighted most of the verses in bright yellow. I pondered those verses and the meaning behind them. Commitments were made to my Heavenly Father through prayer. Nothing else in the book was marked. I pondered the highlighted section. "Dad, is this true?" I opened to the scripture and we talked about it. One of those father-daughter talks that sealed a testimony in my heart. A testimony that would become critical two years later.

My high school boyfriend was not a member of the church. We dated through our first year in college. He asked me to marry him. I accepted the ring – for 24 hours. One of the hardest things I've ever had to do in my life was give it back. Section 132 was engraved on my heart. I wanted a temple marriage. There was no question.

That high school boyfriend eventually desired to learn of my commitment and investigated and joined the church. We've been married for 34 years. The scriptures not only influenced my life, but became the voice above all else which inspired me to chart my own course. Search, ponder and pray. Three simple words which led to my eternal destiny.

Promises and Blessings

The scriptures are a source of answers. My pages are filled with circles and highlights and arrows. Margins are filled with words of testimony and enlightenment. Sometimes a scripture appears as though red blinking lights point to it. More often, a scripture will gently point me in the right direction.

With all of our mortal challenges in this life and with the knowledge we have that the Lord knows everything and how much He loves us, shouldn't we earnestly seek His counsel? Remember – He wants us to succeed. He wants to help us and guide us and protect us. I think the Lord is probably as eager to communicate with us as we are to receive His divine direction. Much of that direction is waiting there within your scriptures. The Lord is just waiting for us to creak open that cover.

As much as I want direction in my own life, I yearn to have it for my children as well. My kids call me their seminary teacher Mom. Though I am no longer serving in that calling in a full-time capacity, I will always be a seminary teacher in my heart. Many times when concerned about one of my children, I have been prompted to open my scriptures. Spiritual nudges led me to read something which directly answered or soothed or gave insight. On some of those occasions I have texted or emailed a scripture to one of my kids. Sometimes it was of temporary comfort. Other times they have told me that it spoke to their soul. One of the best things that we can do as mothers is for our children to know that we love the scriptures. If they know that, they will begin to turn to the scriptures when they grow up.

When we sit down to study the scriptures, we create a holy place. A place where we can learn more about the Lord. A place where we can know Him. A place where we can hear His voice.

I recognize that we are each in a different phase of life. Different seasons of life bring different schedules and priorities. Some of us work at home and have small children running around making life an orchestrated circus. Some of us are in school or work full time with heavy schedules. Some of us are in the midst of health issues which cause physical and mental distraction. There may not be time or energy available to devote a portion of every day to scripture study. All I suggest is that we each do a little better. Start with that. Just a little more time in scriptures will develop into just a little more gospel understanding. That will ultimately become just a little stronger relationship with the Savior. All those "littles" will eventually add up to a lot.

The promises made by the Lord to those who study the scriptures are real.

- <u>We will know and recognize truth</u>. A promised light in a world filled with half-truths and people who deceive. For *"whoso treasureth up my word, shall not be deceived … "* (Joseph Smith-Matthew verse 37).

- <u>We will be inspired to speak the Lord's words</u>. Earthly treasures are fleeting, but the treasures of heaven are eternal in nature and permanent for *"treasure up in your minds continually the words of life, and it shall be given you in the very hour that portion that shall be meted unto every man"* (D&C 84:85).

- <u>There is healing in His words</u>. For we are invited to *"come up hither to hear the pleasing word of God, yea, the word which healeth the wounded soul"* (Jacob 2:8).

The more we can study and read His words, the more we will come to know Him. I have a saying written on the inside cover of my scriptures which motivates me to study. It reads:

Know God	No God
vs.	
Know peace	No peace

There is a difference between knowing God and knowing of Him. Many in the world today know **OF** Him. That is easily attained. Knowing God – a higher level. If we want to know God we must turn to the scriptures to learn and to understand his ways. Bruce R. McConkie said:

"To know God is to think what He thinks, to feel what He feels, to have the power He possesses, to comprehend the truths He understands, and to do what He does. Those who know God become like Him, and have His kind of life, which is eternal life."[9]

We read of further blessings directly related to scripture study in the Book of Mormon. In Mosiah we read the story of the great King Mosiah who gathered all the people of Zarahemla together and read to them the scriptures. He read the records of Zeniff. He read the account of Alma and his brethren. It is remarkable the blessings that came to the people as a result. They were:

- *"struck with wonder and amazement"*
- *"filled with exceedingly great joy"*
- *"thought of their brethren"*
- *"thought of the immediate goodness of God and his power"*
- grateful and *"did raise their voices and give thanks to God"*
- *"filled with … anguish for the welfare of their souls"*

(Mosiah 25:7-11)

These same blessings are available to us today.

What divine direction awaits us in the pages! Years ago a scripture jumped off the page and gave me comfort in the midst of a time when I felt my world was falling apart. At the time I was so concerned about HOW and WHEN life would be okay again. One morning as I read I saw an equation:

"Search diligently, pray always, and be believing, and all things shall work together for your good ... " (D&C 90:24).

It was a mathematical equation for life and was just as true as 1+1=2.

Search diligently + pray always + be believing = it will all work out

As we go about our busy and sometimes difficult lives, let us not forget the power in the pages. Power and enlightenment will inspire us to chart our own course. Power and direction which will keep those grievous wolves away. We wouldn't hike a mountain trail without tools. That cool breeze when hiking – it's a tender mercy. The scriptures are like that cool breeze. They are a tender mercy from the Lord specifically for us. Food for thought. It is time that we "take heed" and feed ourselves.

Chapter 5

True to the Faith

One of the reasons that I loved teaching the Doctrine and Covenants in seminary was the history behind the revelations. The amount of material provided for teaching was overwhelming, but well worth the investment of time. Beyond the scriptures and the lesson manuals was a book that detailed the stories behind the scenes – stories that gave me a glimpse into the heart and soul of the early saints. Stories that made the scriptures come alive for me.

How delightful to join together around the 24th of July to sing praises to the pioneers of old. It is a time to reflect and honor the dedication of those who came before us. It is fun to sing hymns together as a ward which celebrate that pioneer spirit. There are fond memories for me of bonnets and pioneer skirts and other reminders as I celebrated during my childhood years in Primary.

In my older years I have thought differently. When I think of the sacrifice and complete dedication of those early saints, it strikes a deeper chord. Thirty-four years of marriage, four children and four grandchildren later – I've been around the block a few times. I've fallen down and gotten back up many times. Trials should not be compared, but I can't help but believe that the pioneers have me beat – by a long shot. How did they do it? I think of them in all walks of life. There are times when I'm hiking up a particularly difficult stretch and my lungs and legs are burning that I think of them. They not only climbed up the rocky ridges, but they pulled a handcart with them. Or didn't eat the day before. Or buried their children along the way. I am humbled.

Standing on the Shoulders of Giants

What is your own history? It is amazing how protective we feel about our names. There are few things in life which are so closely intertwined with our identities. Names define how we perceive ourselves and are perceived by others. They usually have a deep personal significance. What we know about our names can change us. They have power to sustain us on our journey. And they help us remember who we are.

In the Book of Mormon, Helaman named his two sons Nephi and Lehi (see Helaman 3:21). Helaman knew the power of names and he told them,

"Behold, I have given unto you the names of our first parents ... and this I have done that when you remember your names ye may remember them; and when ye remember them ye may remember their works; and when ye remember their works ye may know ... that they were good. Therefore, my sons, I would that ye should do that which is good" (Helaman 5:6-7).[1]

I remember a day in Grandma C's living room. The year was 1991. I was resting comfortably in a chair. My legs and hips were tired from carrying this baby boy in my belly. Two girls and now a boy on the way. Grandma C did what she did best – tell stories from our ancestors. She began telling me about Percy Edward Austin Chamberlain – my Great Grandma Cederlof's father.

Missionaries appeared at Percy's door. He listened to the message and became converted to the gospel of Jesus Christ. Like many others, he was determined to bring his family to the United States from England in the early 1900s to head West and gather with other saints. After enduring great hardships during their trek westward, his wife died shortly after their arrival in Utah. Percy suffered a broken heart. He had two little daughters to raise by himself. To lose the love of his life after so much sacrifice was more than he could bear. Percy walked five miles up to the cemetery every single day to put fresh flowers on his wife's grave. When despair overtook the better part of him he "took the drink" as they used to say. For a time he was lost. Hope was adrift. The Relief Society helped care for the little girls. They made sure that food was provided.

At some point Percy received a tender mercy. Something from God which caused him to ponder a better life. A life to honor his deceased wife and raise his little girls. In the deepest, darkest moment of his life he stood and looked upward. His faith rose above his grief and he turned his life around. Years later as a proud father of two beautiful daughters, he was admired by all that knew him and of his courageous fight back. A story of inspiration. Grandma C wiped her tears as we sat and pondered his legacy.

Percy Edward Austin Chamberlain. We hadn't yet come up with a name for our boy who would be born a few months later. Austin Chamberlain Tucker. I knew it was right. A fighting, strong spirit who persevered despite tragedy. That was strength and power that I wanted in his name. A heritage to be proud of.

The more connected we feel to our righteous forefathers, the more likely we are to find the strength to make wise and righteous choices. Each of us will be greatly blessed if we know the stories of faith and sacrifice that led our forefathers to endure hardship and stay faithful. "The two-pound coin of the United Kingdom has inscribed on its side 'Standing on the Shoulders of Giants.' When I think of our great pioneer forefathers, I feel that we are all standing on the shoulders of giants."[2]

I love the hymn "True to the Faith." We sing it often at youth firesides and devotionals. The words celebrate the youth and their desire to make righteous choices. But the fourth verse speaks to me of those before us:

We will strive to be found worthy
Of the kingdom of our Lord,
With the faithful ones redeemed
Who have loved and kept his word. Yes!

It is the greatest desire of my heart that I might honor the legacy of my righteous ancestors. They sacrificed their lives and were willing to lay everything on the altar for their faith. Can I look upward and fight the fight as they did? I believe I can. And the more that I know about their stories, the stronger the desire in my heart.

Pleasant Green Taylor was my Great Great Grandfather whose family became the first members of the church in Missouri. They all knew the Prophet Joseph Smith very well. Pleasant's sister became very ill and the family was worried she might die. This sister had great faith and she knew that Joseph Smith could heal her and so the mother sent Pleasant off to run and find the prophet and ask him to hurry back to give his sister a blessing. The prophet was not able to return to the home with Pleasant, so he sent a red silk handkerchief with his blessing and promised that the delivery of this handkerchief was a promise that the girl should get well.

What faith this sister must have had. She received the red handkerchief with the promise of the blessing told by Joseph Smith and she was healed immediately. I can only hope that my faith in the priesthood would be this great if I were ill. My pioneer ancestors were not wealthy, but they possessed strong testimonies and unshakable faith.

After the death of Joseph Smith, Pleasant Green Taylor and his family were present and saw Brigham Young come into the Bowery where the saints had assembled. He and this same sister who had been healed gathered to hear Brigham Young speak. This pioneer family rose to their feet with hundreds of others when before their eyes they saw the spirit of Joseph Smith standing in place of Brigham Young. I know this because they have written in their journals of the unbelievable but certain vision that even after Brigham began to speak, they still thought it was the Prophet Joseph Smith that was speaking to them. This family of pioneer ancestors of mine wrote of their testimonies that Joseph had been resurrected and about the peace that they felt.

This great pioneer family eventually had to leave as the mob forced them from their home. They again experienced miracles along their way. A portion of Pleasant Green Taylor's journal reads:

"The Governor Ford and the mob, demanding that the Saints leave their beautiful city and temple (Nauvoo) so dear to them, we accordingly made preparations to obey this order. And was called upon by Brigham Young to go among the first and pioneer the way. And on the 8 day of February 1846 crossed the Mississippi River on the ice and camped on the Sugar Creek some miles west. Remained here about 2 weeks, weather cold and stormy. We then took up our march and having roads and bridges to construct we were only able to proceed about 3 miles per day. After about a week arrived at Des Moines River. Our food consisted of parched corn and wild onions and while in this condition, the Lord sent a large flock of quails into our camp. Hundreds were gathered up and prepared as food for which we felt very thankful for surely we were needing a change. Brother Brigham took an active part in helping."[3]

What is my heritage? Those before me who witnessed miracles and recorded and bore testimony through their journals. They represent and lived a high level of faith. A level that I aspire to. Their memories and words motivate me to live my life to be deserving of this kind of faith. The kind of faith that precedes miracles.

Orson Pratt was pioneer ancestry on my mother's side. Orson was among those who gathered in the new city of Nauvoo in the 1840s. As a teacher of mathematics and English literature at the University of the City of Nauvoo, he was equaled by few and surpassed by none. Orson's fellow teachers at the University included Sidney Rigdon. Orson's business with the apostles was extensive. He met often with them to issue several epistles to emigrating saints, advocating debt cancellations among the members, additional support for the construction of the temple, and contributions for the settling of converts from abroad.

For 12 years, Orson had been absorbed in the Prophet Joseph Smith and the cause of furthering the gospel of Jesus Christ. In Orson's words we read:

"I ... became intimately acquainted with the Prophet Joseph Smith, and continued ... until the day of his death. I had the great privilege, when I was in from my missions, of boarding the most of the time at his house, so that I not only knew him as a public teacher, but as a private citizen, as a husband and father. I witnessed his earnest and humble devotions both morning and evening in his family. I heard the words of eternal life flowing from his mouth ... I saw his countenance lighted up as the inspiration of the Holy Ghost rested upon him, dictating the great and most precious revelations ... I saw him trans-lating, by inspiration, the Old and New Testaments, and the inspired book of Abraham from Egyptian papyrus. And what is now (1859) my testimony concerning that man, founded upon my own personal observations? It is the same today as if was when I first received the testimony that he was a Prophet. I knew that he was a man of God. It was not a matter of opinion with me, for I received a testimony from the heavens concerning that matter."

As the decision to abandon Nauvoo was made, the temple there was forced to close for a few days. Orson still quietly camped inside the building taking astronomical measurements by night to prepare for the immense job of navigating the pioneers upon departure. He carried these measuring instruments with him as he ventured West with the saints attempting at various points to determine the latitude and longitude in order to keep the migration on course.[4]

What is my heritage? A burning personal testimony and knowl-edge and friendship with the Prophet Joseph Smith. A relationship which burned in hearts and changed their lives forever. Can I not study the words of the prophets and find my own burning desire to know that they are men of God? Can I not sacrifice the time needed to study and develop a level of understanding and testimony that will motivate me to follow the prophets? It is a goal worthy of commitment in honoring my ancestors and God.

In a small village in Sweden in 1861, a mother and father sit by the fire – their hearts heavy. Their daughter, Mary Bjork, had just announced that she was going to America. At 23 years of age she had listened to a "home" missionary, John Cederlof, testify that in a new and far-off land, God the Father and his Son Jesus Christ had appeared to a 14-year old boy named Joseph Smith. Through Joseph Smith this true church had been re-stored to the Earth. It was called The Church of Jesus Christ of Latter-day Saints. Imagine the thoughts and emotion that stirred within this young woman, for she had a new and wonderful religion and she had fallen in love with John. But to leave her family and friends …

And so two young Mormon converts began an adventure that would affect the lives of many others in my family. We know how the father must have felt the day after Mary, his only daughter, left when he went to her room and just stood in the doorway. They say even strong fathers weep when their daughters leave. I think this father wept.

They were on the old sailing boat for nine weeks. The captain of the boat performed the marriage of John and Mary aboard ship, but the jour-ney was long and difficult. Head winds held them up for days, water was short and many of the passengers including Mary were infested with lice. The days were long. The weeks were longer.

Once on shore, John and Mary worked their way West. They were to become pioneers and seasoned frontier people, but not in the begin-ning. They were not used to wagons and oxen, or to living off the country, nor to fording rivers, nor to the hazards of wild Indian tribes. Especially new to them, and probably beyond their imaginations, were the unending stretches of prairie: the heat, and the dust, and the slow tortuous trails over mountain passes. There are rivers to cross. Rain is pouring down, it is cold, and there is no place to stay. No dry clothes. She lay down in the brush, tears mixed with raindrops, while John tried to shelter her from the driving rain.

Mary missed her parents. She wondered if they would eventually come west as well. They would now be new grandparents. Mary delivered Ed, her first baby boy. John built a little cart and they pulled it along with baby and a few personal items in it. They trudged along mile after mile. The sun was hot and bright and the prairie dust was white. A blindness, like snow blindness, came upon Mary and she could scarcely see. She made her way only by watching the coat tail or the rhythmically moving boots of the men walking along ahead of her. Body and mind and spirit were sorely tried.

At long last they came down Parley's Canyon and looked out upon the valley of the Great Salt Lake that was to be their new home. They must have had mixed emotions. Surely the valley was uninviting, but it was home and they could rest. What a great picture it would be, and what I would give, for a glimpse of that young couple, holding their baby and standing by their little cart looking at this desert valley. A long struggle since Sweden.

When John, Mary and little Ed entered the valley they went to the tithing yard where they lived in a cow stall for two weeks. During this time they lived on bread and water. From there they moved to a dugout which was made by digging a hole in the ground and then putting a roof over it which rested on the ground level and sloped up to a low peak in the middle. There were no walls above the ground level. The roof was made of sticks and weeds and then covered with dirt. It leaked badly. When it rained one day outside, it rained two days inside. They had to move little

Ed about so the water wouldn't drip on him.

Mary was a hard worker and did the many things that a good pioneer mother had to do to care for a young and now growing family. She took wool from the sheep, cleaned and carded it, spun it into thread, and made socks and clothes and quilts for her family. She put up salt pork in barrels. She stuffed pig gut and made sausages. She ground wheat in a little hand coffee grinder to make mush. She helped the cows calve. Her refrigerator was a box set in the creek. Midwives brought her children into the world at home.

Eventually Mary's mother and father did decide to come to America. They wanted to be with their daughter and live among the saints. Imagine the feelings of this brave couple, now 54 years old as they left their home and native land to start for a new world and a new life. They crossed the ocean and began to trek across the plains as pioneers on the old trail. But father was not to reach the valley, nor to see his daughter Mary again. He died and was buried on the plains somewhere in Nebraska. What were his last thoughts and how heavy was the heart of mother as she left his crude grave and turned again toward the harsh and endless prairie heading West. Was she sorry she ever left home? She must have dreaded the moment when she would meet Mary and have to tell her that her father lay back on the plains. She would join Mary in the valley and live with them for years before her death.

In January of 1889, Ed fell ill with typhoid fever. He died at the age of 22. This was a cruel blow. Ed would do anything for his mother Mary, and she for him. He was her firstborn son brought into the world under terribly trying conditions. She and John had pulled him across the plains and mountains in the little cart. She had put him to bed in the cow stall. She had shielded him from the rain in the "digout." In the words of my great grandfather, "When Ed died it nearly done mother up." She walked up and down and couldn't sleep. Often she would go down by the creek all alone and sit by the water.

A few years later Mary's youngest son, Albert, was stricken with diphtheria and died. He was 9 years old. Just as Albert died, he put his arms out and said, "There's grandma."

What is my heritage? A strong and loveable woman who had great strength and character. Hers was not a quiet life, but one of action, romance, danger, hard work, dramatic moments, great decisions, sore trials and deep sorrows. Her life was about as humble as a life could be, and yet in looking back on it, what I see is a life of dignity and triumph. She was the virtuous woman of Proverbs for *"who can find a virtuous woman for her price is far above rubies"* (Proverbs 31:10). As one of her descendants I am compelled to *"arise up, and call her blessed"* (Proverbs 31:28). How do my actions and sacrifice compare? How strong is my faith? With my own hardships and choices will my life honor hers? Will I live true to her faith? It is an ongoing journey to do so.[5]

These are my stories. For years I have talked to living relatives and searched through records for the words left by those before. They inspire me. Their blood runs deep in my veins and the more I know about them, the more I love them and feel their strength. I weep for the choices and sacrifices that they made for our family.

You have your own stories – stories which inspire you to a higher calling. You may or may not have a pioneer heritage. But you do have family that once struggled, yet persevered and gave everything for family – for life. Perhaps you are the first to accept the gospel. Your future generations will surely look to you as their own inspiration.

Truthfully, the Mormon pioneer heritage of faith and sacrifice is yours because it is the heritage of The Church of Jesus Christ of Latter-day Saints. For all of us, whether we have Pioneer forefathers or not, a sense of history, an understanding of the difficulties which surrounded the Restoration of the gospel gives us an appreciation for our present blessings and certainly helps us understand our responsibilities.[6]

When teaching the Doctrine and Covenants in seminary I was acutely aware of these present blessings. Often I would sit in church and feel an emotional sense of gratitude for the building, the freedom to worship, the unity as a ward. Early saints in my family line sacrificed everything so that I could worship in an air conditioned building. Often I try to remember the simple things in my gratitude prayers. I am grateful to my Heavenly Father for warm blankets and soft beds and rooftops and raincoats and medicine as my heart and my soul remember those before me.

May I suggest a detour the next time that you find yourself in Salt Lake City: a visit to Temple Square. Take a tour. Look up at the beautiful temple. Tour the visitor's center. Enjoy a recital in the tabernacle, and finish up at the handcart monument. Don't walk too quickly. See the determined face of the father as he strains against the handle of the cart. There is a hole in the knee of his trousers and his shoes are worn. The mother is helping him pull, but is looking backward at her little daughter who rides on the top of the cart. A little boy, maybe 10, is pushing on the back of the cart. The family cooking pot hangs beneath.

What they did, we shall not have to do. What they endured we probably shall not have to endure, nor shall we suffer as they suffered. But let it be said that we have the pioneer spirit. For with it we will be undaunted in our determination to achieve righteousness and accomplish His will.

My father went to visit his mother (Grandma C to me) one day when she was well into her 90s. They decided to go for a short walk. Her joints were painfully swollen from a lifetime of rheumatoid arthritis. This would be a slow walk down to the corner and back – about 200 feet. Grandma C took my dad's arm. They talked about the pioneers. My dad asked her, "Mom, what would you do if the prophet said let's all go to

Jackson County?" Grandma C looked him right in the eye and said, "I'd start."

Grandma C had pioneer spirit. She understood the legacy of family before her and pulled that strength into her own spirit. Despite the hard hikes and the difficulties on the trail before us, do our actions honor those before us? They were the believers.

"Be thou an example of the believers, in word, in conversation, in charity, in spirit, in faith, in purity" (1 Timothy 4:12).

Sometimes we find ourselves on the most difficult of hikes. These are times when prayers are unanswered or not uttered at all. Times when life and emotions are so heightened that nothing makes sense. There appears to be no reason or fairness. Where are the mercies? Perhaps, like Grandma C, we can start. Life wasn't fair for them either. Perhaps we can hold on to the faith of those before. To pull our faces upward and stand on the shoulders of giants.

Beyond the Veil

We've talked about ancestors and loved ones and the strength and fortitude that was represented by their lives here on Earth. Their testimonies and actions spoke volumes about their commitment to faith, love and family. They were truly inspiring. But does their inspiration end with their stories? I don't believe so. Why would a departure from this Earth end a relationship of influence? It doesn't.

"When men are prepared (for death), they are better off to go hence ... The spirits of the just are exalted to a greater and more glorious work; hence they are blessed in their departure to the world of spirits. Enveloped in flaming fire, they are not far from us, and know and understand our thoughts, feelings, and motions, and are often pained therewith."[7]

We read countless accounts of "life after death" experiences. There are books and articles aplenty. People who have died and then been brought back to life by medical means testify of gathering with past loved ones in another sphere. There are many who are critically ill and days before passing will tell family that they saw deceased family members in the room. My daughter Aubreigh is an ICU and ER nurse at the Park City hospital. She has had countless experiences with this. As a critical care giver, she has been present during the passing of many. She testifies firmly of the love and spiritual reality of this beautiful scene of two different worlds coming together for a brief moment. Critics would blame this on hysteria and hallucinations. Certainly we are each allowed our own opinion. I choose to believe in continued relationships.

In my own family there are many. Earlier we read about Mary Bjork's 9-year-old son Albert who was stricken with diphtheria and died. Just as he died, he put his arms out and said, "There's Grandma." This grandma had left her home in Sweden to be with her daughter and grandchildren. She crossed the plains and buried her husband there. She continued to support and encourage this little family as she lived the rest of her life with them in Salt Lake City. Why wouldn't she return to provide comfort and transport to the next life for a little 9-year-old boy? There is love beyond the veil. And what comfort this must have provided to Mary knowing that her little boy would be looked after by Grandma.

My Grandpa Spiker died suddenly in his yard one day while working on the irrigation system. One of the things that he often did was pat his wife (Grandma Spiker) on the hip. It was a small but meaningful little symbol of their love and relationship together. Days after his passing, Grandma Spiker was laying on her side in bed grieving the loss of her husband. She told family the next day that she felt the little familiar "pat" while alone in the room. She knew it was him telling her that everything would be okay. There is comfort beyond the veil.

Two years ago my Uncle Brent suffered a heart attack and had to undergo a quadruple bypass surgery. He survived the surgery, but quickly developed complications with pneumonia. Surgery was performed to reinflate his collapsed lungs. During that surgery he died on the table, but was brought back to life. When he woke from the surgery, he told his wife (Aunt Wendy) that he saw his Mom (Grandma C). Uncle Brent was connected to a respirator because he could not breathe on his own. His arms were restrained and he was heavily medicated with pain and anxiety medication.

The next week things turned bad. His lungs continued to fill up with fluid. Aunt Wendy asked for a priesthood blessing. In the blessing she was told, "Brent has a great work to do." She pondered that phrase for several days in an attempt to understand what that meant. She didn't know if the "work" involved this life or the next. It was very difficult to leave Brent, but she knew that she needed direction from the Lord in the temple. She left Brent's bedside and spent some time in the celestial room. There she received a strong confirming voice which said, "The Lord has called Brent to a greater work in the temples on the other side." He wasn't called by a bishop – he wasn't called by a stake president – this was a calling from the Lord. She left the temple with a strong knowledge that it was time for Brent to go. She now knew that he was needed on the other side.

Aunt Wendy returned to the hospital. She was blessed by a brief 24-hour period where Uncle Brent "woke up" and was able to communicate by mouthing words and writing statements on a chalkboard. She told Brent about the answer she received at the temple. He replied, "I know because my Dad came and already told me and he also said that he received approval to be my escort to the other side." Now they both had a mutual understanding. Brent told Wendy that he loved her and felt bad that she would be left alone with the kids. Wendy promised to live her life worthy of his example.

Brent was able to write a statement on the chalkboard that he did not want to be connected to any machinery which would preserve his life. His lungs continued to fill with fluid and he had to be restrained again. He fell back into a non-communicative state. He would still receive pain and anxiety medication but no further heart or lung support.

Once the machinery was disconnected, Uncle Brent relaxed. His arms were no longer restrained. There was a great peace in the room. Aunt Wendy and her kids gathered around his bedside to talk about fond memories with their dad. He lived for just over 24 hours off the life support. During this 24-hour period, he would suddenly open his eyes and look up at the ceiling. He began mouthing words as if having a conversation with someone that he could see. Wendy whispered in his ear ... "Who are you talking to?" He mouthed the words, "My family." This happened several more times during that peaceful 24-hour period before he passed. There is peace beyond the veil.

Every shepherd knows the names of all his sheep
And not one can come to harm while in his keep
But when they wander from their keeper
Who is there to hold them near?
Do they know that there's no reason for their fear?

For there are angels
Watching o'er the Shepherd's sheep
To warm them in the night and guard their sleep
And there are angels
To hold them through the rain
To guide them safely to the fold again.

If from his nest a sparrow cannot fall
Unnoticed by the Shepherd of us all

Can it be that He's forsaken you
Through the hardships you have known?
Do you know that you will never walk alone?[8]

Alma testifies in the Book of Mormon about angels ministering to us: *"And now, he imparteth his word by angels unto men, yea, not only men but women also. Now this is not all; little children do have words given unto them many times, which confound the wise and the learned"* (Alma 32:23).

As stated by President Joseph F. Smith:

"When messengers are sent to minister to the inhabitants of this earth, they are not strangers, but from the ranks of our kindred, friends, and fellow-beings and fellow-servants. The ancient prophets who died were those who came to visit their fellow creatures upon the earth ... In like manner our fathers and mothers, brothers, sisters and friends who have passed away from this earth, having been faithful, and worthy to enjoy these rights and privileges, may have a mission given them to visit their relatives and friends upon the earth again, bringing from the divine Presence messages of love, of warning, or reproof and instruction, to those whom they had learned to love in the flesh."[9]

Many may wonder the location of the spirit world. Children draw pictures of deceased loved ones up in the clouds of the sky living in heaven. It is a common illustration of their best imagination. President Harold B. Lee gave us some insight:

"Where is the spirit world? Is it away up in the heavens? That isn't what the scriptures and our brethren explain. They have told us the spirit world is right here round about us, and the only spirits who can live here are those who are assigned to fill their missions here on earth. This is the spirit world. And if our eyes could be opened we could see those who have departed from us – a father, mother, brother, a sister, a child. We could see them, and sometimes when our physical senses are asleep, sometimes our spiritual self – and we have ears, spiritual ears, and spiritual eyes – sometimes they will be very keen and awake,

and a departed one may come while we are lying asleep and come into our consciousness. We'll feel an impression. We'll wake up. Where does it come from? It comes from the spirits of those whom we are sealed to."[10]

Austin was having a difficult time in high school. Peer pressure at the age of 17 and making good choices were at battle with one another. His path was unclear and his testimony was shaken. Live for the moment … you only live once … themes of the day were the sounding cry of the typical high school kid. Somebody, however, knew that Austin was better than that.

It was a night not unlike any other. Though this one would be much different and never forgotten. As Austin lay in bed asleep, he had a dream so real that it must have been. Grandma C was there – just sitting at the foot of his bed. But how could she be? She had passed several years before. "Tell me about things, Austin." She was there to love. She was there to listen. He poured his heart out to her. Told her of all the unrest in his soul. She reminded him of his greatness. She reminded him of his potential glory. What his legacy might be. Austin wept.

The next morning would be different. Austin's heart had changed. He thought of the conversation in the night. He would change his course. There is encouragement beyond the veil.

"In the gospel of Jesus Christ you have help from both sides of the veil, and you must never forget that. When disappointment and discouragement strike … you remember and never forget that if our eyes could be opened we would see horses and chariots of fire as far as the eye can see riding at reckless speed to come to our protection."[11]

I know that loved ones who passed are there to celebrate spiritual benchmarks in our life. Just as they mourn our troubles with us, they revel in our joy. Reverent moments when love and righteousness and joy are shared in both spheres.

It was my wedding day. My husband and I were ready to be escorted into the sealing room of the Mesa Arizona Temple. Take a deep breath. Here we go. As I entered the room I quickly looked around to see loved ones present. Family and friends there to support us. I immediately had the feeling that someone was missing. Quickly I looked through the faces. Then a tender mercy. A quiet thought. Grandpa C is here. He had passed away just a year earlier. At this young stage of experience and testimony, I'm so grateful to have recognized it. So sacred and soft I could have missed it. I looked over at Grandma C sitting by herself. But I knew she wasn't alone.

Thirty-two years later I was sitting in the bride's room at the Draper Utah Temple. There were no brides that day and I was waiting there by myself for my daughter Ashlyn. She was receiving her endowments that day and would be married three days later. She and I would meet up in a few minutes and so I took the time to gather my thoughts. I felt the joy of this day. How proud I was of all my children. Grateful for their commitment to the gospel.

And then a sweet, loving voice. "Grandma C is here." It was so real that I pulled my head and gaze upward – looking throughout the room. She was there. I could feel it. She understood my tender feelings of joy that day. That she would come to share it with me brought me to tears. A deep love between us which would unite in a spiritual celebration of significance. Our hearts together understood the importance. There is sentiment beyond the veil.

True to the faith. What does that mean to you? You decide. You know the legacy before you. Dig down deep to your family's roots and honor that. Follow the footprints left for you.

True to the faith. It means beginning where theirs ended and forming your own footprints for still others to one day follow. Their legacy may be a sliver of hope for you. Hope that you too can move forward. Come what may ... all is well.

Chapter 6

Messenger of Hope

Hope. You can see it. You can hear it. You can feel it. We are desperate to find it. Its presence can be fleeting – just a small moment. A gift from Heavenly Father. A sign that He knows you and your troubles. An assurance that you matter.

Let us remind ourselves of the Plan. We came here to Earth to succeed in returning to live with our Heavenly Father. And we voted for it! We all raised our hands in support of it. There were two things that we knew. One – we wanted bodies. Two – we knew that there would be struggles through which we would learn and grow stronger. Why would we vote for struggles? Because we knew there was a gift which would be a key to our success here on Earth. The gift of the Holy Ghost. Key because it would help us on our journey to know God's will for us. We would not be left alone.

Elder Parley P. Pratt gives a beautiful description of the effects of the Holy Ghost:

"(His influence) quickens all the intellectual faculties, increases, enlarges, expands and purifies all the natural passions and affections; and adapts them, by the gift of wisdom, to their lawful use. It inspires, develops, cultivates and matures all the fine-toned sympathies, joys, tastes, kindred feelings and affections of our nature. It inspires virtue, kindness, goodness, tenderness, gentleness and charity. It develops beauty of person, form and features. It tends to health, vigor, animation and social feeling. It invigorates all the faculties of the physical and intellectual man. It strengthens, and gives tone to the nerves. In short,

it is, as it were, marrow to the bone, joy to the heart, light to the eyes, music to the ears, and life to the whole being."[1]

Are we using this gift to its potential? When a child's baptism and confirmation are performed on the same day, the confirmation sometimes is treated like a routine, perfunctory middle step between the much-anticipated baptism and the subsequent family gathering to celebrate. The ordinance where the promised companionship of the godhead's third member is given and inspired blessings are pronounced by a Melchizedek Priesthood holder deserves better.

The Holy Ghost can provide a fullness of the blessings from the Spirit's constant companionship in your life. This is a fulfillment of the Savior's promise:

"And I will pray the Father, and he shall give you another Comforter, that he may abide with you forever" (John 14:16).

Baptism is a singular event. But this Holy Ghost is the medium by which we receive inspiration, personal revelation, witnesses, comforts and cautions – not just once or occasionally, but day to day as we live worthily and seek such promptings.[2] This is our own personal guide to hope. To recognize it. To embrace it. And it is not meant to be complicated. Nephi confirms:

"For my soul delighteth in plainness ... For the Lord God giveth light unto the understanding; for he speaketh unto men according to their language, unto their understanding" (2 Nephi 31:3).

We all learn in different ways. The promise from God is that the Holy Ghost will speak to each of us in our own way of learning. It is imperative that each of us take a true look at ourselves and recognize how and where and when do we feel the Spirit best? What puts you in tune to your own personal revelation? How do you hear that whisper?

The scriptures often use the word voice to describe the Spirit. The delicate, fine spiritual communications are not seen with our eyes nor heard with our ears, but rather a voice that one *feels* more than *hears*. This voice of the Spirit is described in the scriptures as being neither loud nor harsh, not a voice of thunder, neither a voice of great tumultuous noise, but rather as still and small, of perfect mildness, as if it had been a whisper and it can pierce even the very soul and cause the heart to burn. It does not get our attention by shouting. It whispers. It caresses so gently that if we are preoccupied, we cannot feel it at all.[3] A missed opportunity. A missed blessing.

Find Your Space

The world is getting brighter, louder and busier. It demands our attention. If we desire stimulation it is there 24-7. Even if we are alone, we can be tuned in with handheld devices, laptops and television to keep us entertained and occupied. Smartphones are a blessing, but they can also distract us from hearing the "still, small voice." This presents a great challenge to feeling the Spirit in our lives. These handheld devices need to be our servants, not our masters. Satan will tempt us in the smallest ways to overschedule our lives. If our lives are too busy and too loud, we are far less likely to feel the Spirit. Satan needs to block this most important form of communication.

We can help others best if we learn to keep our own emotional well-being intact and guard our spirit. Think of your spirit as your inner flame – a candle burning brightly at the core of your being. Just as you may need to guard a real candle's flame with your hand, you may also need to protect your spirit. When mine is in jeopardy or has been drowned out by the noise of the world, I feel scattered and unable to access my inner source of wisdom and peace. Realize that when your flame is low, you aren't capable, emotionally and spiritually, to deal with problems. Each of us must find our own way to nourish our flame. To keep our candle burning bright.[4]

We must find personal quiet time. We all need time to meditate and contemplate. Even Jesus Christ, during His mortal ministry, found time to do so:

"And when he had sent the multitudes away, he went up into a mountain apart to pray: and when the evening was come, he was there alone" (Matthew 14:23).

Some would call it a matter of balance in your life. I personally don't think I really ever have a totally balanced day – ever. Life pulls on me in a variety of directions depending on what is happening with my family, my job, my church calling, etc. Each day is different and varied. To me it is more about priorities. I need to ask myself – regardless of what else happened today, did I set aside time to hear the heavenly words "be still, and know that I am God?"[5]

As a reminder of this, I typed up a statement and placed it next to my computer at home. It is something that I see and read every day. Something that I need as a "Type A" personality who can fill my days with "stuff." A reminder to prioritize and do what it takes to facilitate that spiritual communication:

*"**BE STILL** (an intentional choice to be calm, be humble, patient, submissive, contrite and receptive to the Holy Ghost) **AND** (then I will pour down knowledge, insight, blessings, power, protection and miracles to such an extent that you will) **KNOW THAT I AM GOD**"* (D&C 101:16, Psalms 46:10; D&C 101:16; D&C 121; D&C 123:17; Exodus 14:13).

The Hebrew base that is translated as *still* in this scripture means "stop, cease your own human striving and watch the Lord do His work." The dictionary states that "still" actually comes from a base meaning "standing" or "immobile." The Lord is saying, "Be immobile and be unwavering. Put your complete trust in the Lord and live."[6]

During the time that Joseph Smith was in the jail at Liberty, Missouri, he wrote words reflecting the importance of standing still:

"*. . . Let us cheerfully do all things that lie in our power; and then may we stand still, with the utmost assurance, to see the salvation of God, and for his arm to be revealed*" (D&C 123:17).

This was written during times of great distress. The Saints were being persecuted and Joseph Smith was imprisoned and surely had desperate and hopeless moments of grief. Within this period he recognized the need to fine tune to the Spirit. It was the doorway to an eternal perspective. A doorway to hope.

Joseph Smith had found this doorway earlier in his life. In his great faith and belief that God would answer his question he found his place to "be still." A place where he could be alone with God. Another prophet, the brother of Jared, was also impelled by his great faith to turn to the Lord to receive guidance. He needed direction for his people – language, land and light. He also sought a place to "be still." Each prophet secluded himself from other people in order to plead with the Lord – one in a grove, the other upon a mountain.[7]

Find your space. Pray to find it. A place where your mind can "be still" and recognize promptings. As I have prayed and spent count-less hours working on finding my space, some predictable patterns have emerged. My sacred place is hiking. My body is not still, but my mind is. It is open and ready for two-way communication. The combination of prayer and the beauty of nature feeds my soul. My 3-mile power prayer walks also serve me well! My arms and legs are pumping hard, but my mind is deep in prayer and pondering. A third pattern is sleeplessness or an awakening in the night. I used to get really angry about not being able to return to sleep after a sudden awakening at 2:00 a.m. After several signifi-cant promptings during those wee hours I now recognize that it is a perfect time for Heavenly Father to get my attention. When I roll over and the clock reads something ridiculous in the middle of the night, I now just begin to pray. We have a conversation. And I am ready and willing to listen.

There are other places that I can quiet my mind and prepare to receive. Talks in sacrament meeting. Lessons in Relief Society or gospel doctrine. Listening to beautiful music. Listening to general conference. It is more than just being there in attendance. It is consciously creating your own space with a prayer in your heart that you'll be ready. Ready in your space to find hope.

The Ultimate Teacher

I loved my calling as a seminary teacher. What better way to spend your early mornings than surrounding yourself with teenagers and telling Book of Mormon stories. It's a little like Primary on steroids. You've got your stories and teachings from the scriptures and artwork on the walls and board all mixed in with high school kids living their own reality. Add to that a dose of teenage hormones and attitude and it's terrific! Definitely put a smile on my face every morning.

I didn't always have a smile on my face. When I was first called to accept the responsibility of an early morning seminary teacher, I smiled and nodded yes with that kind of deer-in-the-headlights look. I still had the smile on my face when I went over to Institute for a special training class for seminary teachers about a month before I started teaching. When I came out of that class – the smile was gone.

Responsibilities were outlined along with other reading materials and class objectives and expectations. For the first time I was really overwhelmed at the amount of knowledge that I thought I needed to know and the expert that I felt I needed to be – and wasn't. I climbed into my car in the parking lot at the end of my first training session and cried. I cried all the way home. My desire to teach and my love for the gospel and for teenagers was strong, but I felt like a failure because I knew that I wasn't an expert scriptorian. I didn't feel like I knew the scriptures forward and backward and would never be able to deliver. What I did not understand then was the key ingredient in teaching that would fill all my inadequate gaps. I turned to the scriptures for support and solace and the Lord showed me this scripture:

"But if ye will turn to the Lord with full purpose of heart, and put your trust in Him, and serve Him with all diligence of mind, if ye do this, He will, according to his own will and pleasure, deliver you out of bondage" (Mosiah 7:33).

A start for me. Heavenly Father has my heart and my trust. I still had the fear. Fear and my own insecurity was my bondage. I continued to search the scriptures. Then I found the key to deliverance out of my own sense of bondage and filling in where I fell short. In Mosiah I read where Alma and his followers are hiding from King Noah and Alma is attempting to set up the church of Christ in the wilderness. Alma is new to this. The priests are new to this. What an overwhelming task for these new priests to teach. I could relate. And Mosiah 18:26 reads:

"And the priests were not to depend upon the people for their support; but for their labor they were to receive the grace of God that they might wax strong in the Spirit, having the knowledge of God, that they might teach with power and authority from God."

That's it! The key principle which will fill my realized and unrealized gaps in my pursuit of becoming a teacher is the Spirit. As a lifelong member of The Church of Jesus Christ of Latter-day Saints, this should have been obvious to me. But it took this particular calling for me to get on my knees, get off my knees and work as hard as I could – and then get back on my knees again.

Many of you have served in leadership and teaching positions in various auxiliaries of the church. You know that the guidelines and outlines of the church for teaching responsibilities used to be far more structured.

The new curriculum is beautiful and inspired and represents a higher level of instruction. We are to study and learn and know the material to be covered, yet be a kind of facilitator. It is our job to present and then lead the discussion, which involves the students. As they answer questions and discuss the material presented, the Spirit will be the ultimate teacher. The learning will take place in the students' hearts. Just as the bar has been raised for missionaries, we are seeing evidence that the bar has been raised in teaching and leadership.

My daughter Aubreigh served for a time in the Stake Relief Society presidency in Provo, Utah. She was able to attend a training session with the general presidency of the Relief Society. In trying to impress and inspire a higher level of leadership, one speaker from that conference reminded those in attendance that this is the Lord's church – not Salt Lake City's church. She cautioned that the gospel is not about the rules of the church. The gospel is about Heavenly Father's children. The advisement was to stop looking to Salt Lake City for the exact outline and start looking to the Spirit for answers.

So, what are some things that we can do in order to really teach with the Spirit? To ensure that the "Ultimate Teacher" – the Spirit – will be in attendance. Many of us hope to be better teachers. Elder Richard G. Scott of the Quorum of the Twelve said:

"I am convinced that there is no simple formula or technique that would immediately allow you to master the ability to be guided by the voice of the Spirit. Our Father expects you to learn how to obtain that divine help by exercising faith in Him and His Holy Son, Jesus Christ. They know that essential personal growth will come as you struggle to learn how to be led by the Spirit."[8]

To me that states that the first step in teaching by the Spirit is to **believe** that we can. To have faith. It is having a testimony and knowing and trusting that Heavenly Father cares enough about what you are teaching to allow the gift of the Holy Ghost to work through you. It is an understanding between you and Heavenly Father that says that you know that it is Heavenly Father's work. When His work gets done, then we all feel the love of Christ.

The second step. **Prepare.** Revelation occurs when you make yourself available to the Lord. When you prepare, the Spirit can speak to you. If you go in unprepared, the Spirit cannot direct you because you have no direction.

Some of my seminary teacher friends and I have a common saying that goes something like this. Prepare and prepare and prepare and let go.

I never knew what awaited me at 6:00 each morning. The hours and the energy that I had spent preparing for the following day were critical. Sometimes I would feel the strongest impression to cover a certain block of scripture or go a certain direction with my thoughts. The ideas would come so fast in preparing that my hand could hardly keep up in writing as fast as the thoughts were coming. Sometimes I would come to class prepared with a lesson that unexpectedly took a very different direction than I had anticipated. And sometimes I would end up teaching a principle that appeared nowhere in my notes. It was humbling to say the least. I knew that I was only a chess piece waiting for the Spirit to make the next move.

There are seminary moments and conversations that I cherish and that have strengthened my testimony. I had seen such growth in the students and felt connections and breakthroughs with each of them individually. There is one day though that I will never forget.

As a new teacher in my first year, I was preparing a lesson for the following day and had studied the scriptures and suggested lesson outlines thoroughly. In trying to wrap it up I felt very strongly inspired to go in a certain direction and the words I knew I needed to say were strong and unmistakable. I don't even remember now what they were. But I knew that night that one of my students needed those words.

When my alarm clock went off at 4:30 a.m. the following morning, the first thing that flooded my mind were those same words. I thought to myself, "Wow – this needs to be said." I prayed that morning that I might be able to deliver to my students what the Lord wanted. Class went well. I thought the Spirit was strong and the kids left for the high school. I remember telling the other seminary teacher of my experience that morning and we both wondered why and who.

Later that afternoon when I was taking my daughter Ashlyn to her high school soccer practice she turned to me in the car and said, "Mom, you know all that stuff you were talking about in seminary today? Well … was that in the lesson manual?" I told her "No, that was something that the Spirit really prompted me to teach." She then told me that the words meant more to her than anything and that she would never forget them. She was my "hope" that day. Hope in learning how to be a better teacher. Hope that gave me the confidence to push forward in this new and demanding calling in the church. Hope in understanding that the Spirit was my partner in this.

The final step – **prayer**. This is best described by President Boyd K. Packer of the Quorum of the Twelve. He stated:

"Learn to pray. Pray often. Pray in your mind, in your heart. Pray on your knees. Prayer is your personal key to heaven. The lock is on your side of the veil."[9]

Perhaps some of you are saying to yourself, "I'm not a teacher. I don't teach seminary or Sunday School or any other class in the church." May I suggest that we are all teachers. Many of us are moms and dads who have young and older children that only we can reach. We are home teachers and visiting teachers. We are a friend. We are missionaries.

There is no parenting class, no Communications 101 class, no friendship manual and no missionary how-to list which can comprehensively instruct you as to how and what to say at a particular time of need. I can tell you firsthand as a seminary teacher and as a parent of four children that our kids are attending school in a war zone. Satan is cleverly masking sin in all kinds of forms and rationalizations. How do we parent that? Live the gospel, set the example, become involved in our children's lives and pray with all our heart for the Spirit to prompt with effective teaching moments. How do we help our friends who have landed themselves in bad situations? Live the gospel, set the example, serve them and pray with all your heart for the Spirit to help you find the right words of comfort and hope. Every member a missionary? Sure – if you know who to teach. The Spirit can help with that.

This "Ultimate Teacher" can be the guide in hiking the trail of your life. He knows all the trails and the dangers and the tools to succeed. It is our responsibility to allow Him to lead. How grateful I am that in a life full of trials and distractions and chaos on those difficult hikes that Heavenly Father has given us one sure thing that will keep our focus toward Him. The Spirit will guide us and others toward eternal life. The "Ultimate Teacher" is a messenger of hope.

Refuge From the Storm

One of the best places to connect with the Spirit is in the temple. The temple is the only "university" for us to prepare spiritually for our graduation to eternal life.[10] Elder David B. Haight said:

"The moment we step into the house of the Lord, the atmosphere changes from the worldly to the heavenly. ... It is a refuge from the ills of life and a protection from the temptations."[11]

There is a poem written by President Spencer W. Kimball for the dedication of the Washington D.C. Temple. It is displayed there in the temple and says:

Enter this door as if the floor were gold.

And every wall of jewels. All of wealth untold.
As if a choir in robes of fire were singing here.
Nor shout nor rush but hush ... for God is here.

What a beautiful reminder of the blessing that is ours to walk out of the world and into God's house. His house confirms that we truly are "A Child of God." It is a vital part of discovering our nobility. Regular attendance at the temple gives us a clearer perspective of the Plan and our divine potential in it. We gain a greater understanding of the Atonement and what it means in our life. It is making a commitment to God that demonstrates your sacrifice and willingness to do what it takes to return to live with Him.

Often we return to the temple to seek guidance in an everyday need such as, "What is the best direction for this talk that I've been asked to give?" Or, "Who should serve alongside me in this new calling that I've received?" Other times we seek direction regarding decisions that are of more eternal consequence, such as, "Is this college major the best choice for fulfilling my potential?" or "Is this job opportunity the right match for me?" or "How can I love this family member without judgment?" Irrespective of the question, the Lord ultimately will provide an answer that will lead us toward the destiny He has planned for us.

President Hinckley said, *"I hope you are using the temple constantly, because you will gain blessings there that you cannot gain anywhere else on the face of the whole earth."*[12]

There are many blessings for each of us in attending the temple. We will always be blessed for our obedience to God. And the spirit found in the temple stays with us as we return to our homes feeling that much closer to God. There are some blessings, however, which are particularly tender for those of us in trying circumstances. These are the days when our hike leads us to the temple for refuge. We are turning events and people in our lives over to the Lord. We recognize that a higher power is needed. These blessings are many. Here are just a few:

- <u>Assurance of Resurrection</u>. One of the paramount questions of this life is, "Will we live again?" It is hoped for by many, ridiculed by some and is passed over by others. But we who come to the temple have access to the world's best teaching of this principle. From the moment you enter the temple, the emphasis is on life eternal. The Resurrection is a recurrent theme that is taught as a reality in all phases of the temple presentation. One cannot participate in temple functions and not come away with an assurance that we will truly live again.
- <u>The cleansing of the soul</u>. The endowment provides that cleansing and the support to continue in that capacity. Each time we come to the temple, whatever rough spots we have accumulated are honed and smoothed by the service we render there.
- <u>Sealing of loved ones</u>. One of the greatest blessings of all is the sealing of families. Not only can we claim them beyond this life, but the assurance of an eternal relationship causes us to be more loving, more concerned for each other –

  it lasts longer than a mere lifetime.
- <u>The touching of family by our attendance</u>. Even the youngest mind among our children and grandchildren understands the significance of going to the temple. The aura that surrounds the temple goer is real, and the fact that we are worthy to enter the house of the Lord is not lost on those we love. What a wonderful legacy to leave behind for I want my children to go to the temple.
- <u>Act of charity</u>. Every time we come to the temple, we commit what President Hinckley calls one of the greatest acts of charity we can do in this life. Being a consistent temple attender requires us to consistently be doing charitable acts. I am not sure that I would be

able to be consistent in my acts of love for others, except for this opportunity.

- <u>A shield and a protection</u>. As part of the endowment, we are given a shield that helps us from being destroyed by him who opposes the Father's Plan. If we honor it and remember that it is a gift from God, we will not be overcome.

- <u>Association with the best people of the Earth</u>. Some of the finest people this world has to offer come through the doors of the temple. None of us are perfect, but we are trying to be like the Savior. This sets us apart from the world and allows for the Spirit of the Lord to function in the temple with us. Someone once said, "We are known by the company we keep." I hope this is true, because the company we keep in the temple is sweet and wonderful.

- <u>Focus on eternal things</u>. We live in a world where the emphasis is on temporary things. There is one place that deals with eternal things and the focus of the mind is on the spiritual rather than the material. That place is the temple. How glad we should be to frequently be exposed to the real rather than the illusory.

- <u>A house of revelation</u>. There are so many confinements to our thought processes. We are just not capable of solving all the intricate and devious problems of life. We need help from some source that has the ability to see beyond our own myopic vision of things.

- <u>Closest place to heaven</u>. The temple is a place where no bad words, thoughts or deeds occur. The hush of spiritual things replaces the clang and dissonance of the daily battle of life. Things are neat and clean. Peace and quiet give rise to innermost feelings and thoughts. Things we participate in have permanent and perpetual consequences rather than things we usually participate in that pass away. It is the nearest thing to heaven that exists on Earth. If you want a taste of celestial life – go to the temple.

- <u>In the presence of Jehovah</u>. The Prophet Habakkuk states, *"The Lord is in His Holy Temple"* (Habakkuk 2:20). It is the goal of all of us to someday be in His presence. Undoubtedly our attendance there will prepare us to be more completely at home with Him. The environment of the temple will quicken our spiritual selves to that eventual hoped-for experience of being with Him eternally.

Elder Vaughan J. Featherstone spoke these words:

"The season of the world before us will be like no other in the history of mankind. Satan has unleashed every evil, every scheme, every blatant, vile perversion ever known to man in any generation. Just as this is the dispensation of the fullness of times, so it is also the dispensation of the fullness of evil. We and our wives and husbands, our children and our members must find safety. There is no safety in the world; wealth cannot provide it, enforcement agencies cannot assure it, membership in this Church alone cannot bring it. As the evil night darkens upon this generation, we must come to the temple for light and safety. In our temples we find quiet, sacred havens where the storms cannot penetrate to us."[13]

If you do not qualify for a temple recommend right now, I suggest that you visit the temple grounds. Nothing prevents you or anyone else from simply visiting the temple grounds. The Lord wants each of us to prepare ourselves to be worthy of a temple recommend and to come to the temple as soon as we can. Walking the beautiful grounds at the temple will plant in your heart a desire to get a recommend and attend the temple as soon as possible.

Satan, on the other hand, does not want you to go to the temple or even to stand in the shadow of the temple. He wants you to avoid even getting close to the temple because he knows the temple is the house of the Lord.

As you go to the temple or visit the temple grounds, you will walk on sacred and holy ground just as the early patriarchs and matriarchs did so long ago. They were focused on their eternal journey and the important things of life. Like them, you also can focus on feeling power and the presence of heaven.[14]

Recently, President Thomas S. Monson made a visit here in Arizona. He came to dedicate the Gilbert Arizona Temple. During the dedicatory prayer he asked the Lord, "May Thy Holy Spirit dwell here, and may its influence be felt by all who come within these walls." He also prayed: "May this, Thy house, be a sanctuary of serenity, a refuge from the storms of life and the noise of the world. May it be a house of quiet contemplation concerning the eternal nature of life and of Thy divine plan for us."[15]

We all need a place to escape the darkness of despair and burdens in our lives. There is a place. A place to pray and to ponder. A place to be heard. A place of hope.

A Guard Against Adversity

Joy is a gift of the Spirit. We are sincerely, wholesomely happy and at peace in our innermost hearts only as we allow ourselves to be led by light. In the Harry Potter series, Albus Dumbledore explains in his wisdom, "Happiness can be found, even in the darkest of times, if one only remembers to turn on the light."[16]

This light is implanted within. This light leads to truth. The Spirit tells us with a flutter or a burning in our heart which confirms that what we are hearing is good and righteous and true. These whispers in our ear or thoughts in our mind are promptings from the Holy Ghost which take us in a certain direction for good. It is a blessing to recognize and use this great influence.

Just as our minds and hearts can be fine-tuned to respond to the promptings of the light, they can also be alerted to potential danger or detrimental choices. I am never excited for opposition, but am grateful that we can feel that darkness when something is not right. I am grateful that the Holy Ghost will place words or thoughts in our mind that will help to get us out of a situation that is dangerous physically or spiritually. The more that we practice listening, the better we will be at recognizing it and reacting to it.

My daughter Aubreigh was on her way to work one day. She works as an ER nurse at a hospital. She had just met her husband for lunch and was headed up the canyon to the hospital. She had recently ordered a new cellphone and the store had called earlier that day to say that the phone was ready for pickup. "Go get the phone." The thought was persistent. Aubreigh thought otherwise. She would get the phone the next day when she wasn't scheduled for work. The phone could wait. The hospital was expecting her that afternoon. "Go get the phone." Again and again. She pulled up to the hospital staff parking and put the car in park. "Go get the phone." A simple thought. She looked at the clock in her car. It was 2:30 p.m. Aubreigh considered the thought. Perhaps she could run over and pick up the phone and add some time to the end of her shift that day. She put the car in reverse, backed out of her spot and drove down the road leading to town.

When Aubreigh returned an hour later there were fire engines, ambulances and police cars. She panicked. "What happened while I was gone?" she thought. Already dressed in scrubs, she ran for the entrance and spoke to one of the emergency personnel. "What happened?" she said. "There was an explosion right here," he pointed. A pipe had exploded above the ceiling at the hospital ER entrance. Pieces of pipe and shrapnel and solid wood beams that had been blown apart were piled on the floor in a flood of water. "Was anybody hurt?" Aubreigh questioned. "Nobody was at the doors when it happened," replied the emergency personnel. "It's a good thing – somebody would have been killed."

The Spirit quietly spoke. Aubreigh knew immediately that she had been warned and saved. She describes it as a quick tornado of events racing through her brain. That persistent thought all the way to work – looking at the clock – the seemingly ridiculous decision to leave and go pick up the phone. She ran inside and found a manager. The video cameras are positioned on the entrance. She already knew, but wanted to see it. She told the manager, "Pull the video. I want to see the time of the explosion." They watched: 2:32 p.m. Aubreigh would have been walking in those doors at that exact time.

The Spirit. A guardian against adversity – or worse. It wasn't her time. This would not be her trial – or our family's. Yes, there will be trials and uphill battles in our lives which are necessary for us to climb and grow from. Aubreigh will face situations in her future which will test her physically and spiritually there is no doubt. But there are moments when the Spirit can speak to us as if to say, "Not this time." It is a gift.

Aubreigh and I have talked many times about this incident. We marvel at the differences in which the Spirit gets our attention. Most often it is a quiet thought. Something that could be easily missed or cast aside. Occasionally it is a strong, forceful impression that stops us in our tracks. And other times a visual impression or message in our mind.

The Comforter

All of us encounter disappointment in our lives. It might come through such circumstances as unmet expectations for ourselves or our loved ones. A child who has strayed. It might be unmet college plans or career opportunities. A job loss or change. It might be hurt feelings from friendship failures or gossip. Feeling shut out. There are many. Sometimes those disappointments are self-induced by setting unrealistic or unattainable goals. Oftentimes it may be out of our control because the actions or inactions of others has an effect or some influence on our lives. Either way the result is despair.

We can find comfort in the midst of disappointment as it was never intended that we go about it alone. The Lord has promised,

"And now, verily I say unto you, and what I say unto one I say unto all, be of good cheer, little children; for I am in your midst, and I have not forsaken you" (D&C 61:36).

My daughter Ashlyn was sitting in front of the temple one evening. She was there seeking comfort. She was feeling lonely and overwhelmed about current conditions in her life. College was difficult and changes were taking place that left her discouraged and disheartened. She just needed to be closer to God and so she took a seat in the beautiful gardens outside the temple. Ashlyn began to pray. She talked to Heavenly Father about her feelings. She prayed that she would feel loved. When she said, "Amen," a text came into her phone.

I was lounging on the couch at home watching a movie with my husband. The thought came. Text Ashlyn. That was all. I reached for my phone. I texted a message about my love for her and what a blessing it was that my kids are also my best friends. A simple heartfelt text.

Ashlyn describes it as a huge moment. Clearly the Lord knew she needed some comfort. The Holy Ghost confirmed to Ashlyn that He was aware. That she was loved. The beauty of it was that she understood in that moment that it wasn't just about a mother's love that lifted her Spirit, but God's love. The Comforter. What a gift. We are not alone.

Can you hear the prayer of the children?
On bended knee, in the shadow of an unknown room
Empty eyes with no more tears to cry
Turning heavenward toward the light.

Crying Jesus, help me

To feel the sun again upon my face,
For when darkness clears I know you're near,
Bringing peace again.[17]

Sometimes we find ourselves in desperate situations. Circumstances may be such that we have lost control of people, places or things! Our heart races as we attempt to get control. With a quick prayer in our heart, do we listen for the Comforter? Can you recognize His voice?

My daughter Amber had just finished her weekly grocery shopping. She was holding her 2-year-old in her arms pushing the grocery cart in the parking lot toward her car. Her 3-year-old was walking alongside the cart holding on with his hand. All of a sudden without any warning, a car screeched into reverse, backed into her cart and took off. The groceries went flying and so did her little boy. He had scraped up knees and a bloody lip. Both children were screaming from fright. The store manager rushed outside after being told of the incident and called the police. Amber tried to remain calm, but wondered how she could even concentrate to give the report to the police officer with both children still crying. And then the Comforter impressed – call your visiting teacher. Amber recognized it. She pulled out her cellphone.

Amber quickly described the conditions and her location to her visiting teacher and wondered if she was able to help. Her visiting teacher was there within the minute because she was doing her own grocery shopping inside the same store. Amber's kids know her visiting teacher and so she was able to calm them while Amber spoke with the officer. A beautiful example of love and service and comfort.

In my seminary class, the students would share their "missionary moments" each Friday. These were situations during the week that they found themselves sharing the gospel. These students had to be ready at all times. Questions were asked and discussions and testimonies shared at school, on sports fields, at friends' houses, on airplanes, and about a hundred other locations. At a moment's notice they might be explaining our beliefs with regard to the Plan of Salvation or who is this Joseph Smith guy or questions about whether or not we believe in Jesus Christ. These are high school kids who desire to engage in these kind of conversations, yet tremble at the thought of being able to recall gospel principles in a snap.

As they testified over and over again on those "missionary moment" Fridays, we all began to know and to trust that the Comforter filled in where we lacked. I saw a transformation from fear of not knowing it all – to faith that it always worked out.

"And now, behold, my beloved brethren, I suppose that ye ponder somewhat in your hearts concerning that which ye should do after ye have entered in by the way. But, behold, why do ye ponder these things in your hearts?"

"Do ye not remember that I said unto you that after ye had received the Holy Ghost ye could speak with the tongue of angels? And now, how could ye speak with the tongue of angels save it were by the Holy Ghost?" (2 Nephi 32:1-2)

The Comforter. Testimonies reinforced over and over again in seminary. Showing us that an eager mind and heart's desire to honor Him is enough.

As our awareness of the Spirit grows and our inner self gains strength, we begin to emphasize a principle that Elder Marvin J. Ashton calls "the time is now." If we have allowed our inner self to become distant, then we find that we often procrastinate – we put things off. I'll make that phone call tomorrow or I'll check on that sister later this week on a less busy day.

Elder Ashton says that to live more fully each hour and to glean the most from each day is wisdom. We are fooling ourselves if we believe that the best of life is just around the corner. When I go on a mission – after marriage – after the house is paid for – after the recession is over – after the children are raised. The best of life is now. Today is the time to really start living. Today is the time to start on tomorrow. The future belongs to those who know how to live now. There are no unimportant days in the lives of those who are anxiously engaged and living in the present.

"For behold, this life is the time for men to prepare to meet God; yea, behold the day of this life is the day for men to perform their labors" (Alma 34:32).

Each of us faces adversity on a large and small scale. It is the way by which we grow and develop and in fact strive toward that perfection that is discussed in the scriptures. The rate at which we grow and how we handle that adversity depends on our inner resources, our drive and diligence. If we were to procrastinate every response to the voice of the Spirit telling us to take action until our lives were running smoothly and perfectly, then we would never take action. Are we committed and diligent in our role as a disciple of Christ? Sure – on those easy hiking trails. But on the difficult? We must always be a disciple – regardless of the trail.

In recalling some of the Savior's well-known teachings, the word now can be appropriately added to emphasize their impact. "If ye love me, keep my commandments," NOW (John 14:25). "Go ye into all the world, and preach the gospel to every creature," NOW (Mark 16:15). "Come, follow me," NOW (Luke 18:22). If we love God, we will serve him – NOW.

There are those among us, though they would deny it, who are hungry for fellowship and activity in the church today. They need us and we need them. It is our duty and blessing to help them find the way – NOW. We and they are God's sheep and we can best be fed and led together. Today is the time to let them know we care and that the Lord loves them.[18]

My dad had a friend years ago who was the captain of a fire station. One day he went down to visit his friend. In their conversation, my dad learned that there was a young woman in a wheelchair who frequently visited the station looking for help. She was essentially homeless – moving from place to place. The captain was worried about her. The winter mornings were cold and she had no coat.

My dad called me at my work that afternoon. "Can you take some time off work this afternoon to come help me out with something?" I arranged to quickly meet my dad. We went to where the fire captain thought she would be. She was brought into our home. My mom and I bathed her. We washed her hair and her clothes. I found an extra coat in my closet that would fit her. My dad and I took her back to a place where she would have some shelter. Dad handed her a wad of bills. He spoke quietly to others at the shelter. "Watch over her," he said.

I saw her weeks later boarding a bus downtown. The wheelchair lift on the city bus was lifting her up. I recognized her because she was wearing my coat.

My dad understands that there is an urgency today for all of us to take time for God. To take time now – not tomorrow. When the Spirit speaks, we must respond as his disciples. We are His hands. There may be someone in your path that needs comforting. The Spirit communicates that need and it is up to us to act now.

Last summer I was walking up and down Main Street in Park City, Utah, with my dad. We were browsing through the shops, enjoying the beautiful cool weather and looking for a place to eat some lunch. We found ourselves in the "Family Tree Center" there on Main Street. It is a visitor's center which encourages people on the street to come in and learn more about their ancestors. There are full-time missionaries who staff the center.

We walked in and were approached by a young sister missionary. She gave a short introduction about the Family Tree Center and an invitation to search for our ancestors or to learn more about the church. We quickly informed her that we were members of the church and introduced ourselves. My dad asked her where she was from. "Panama," she said with a smile. She was thrilled to be serving a mission. "What about your family?" asked my dad. "They are not members. They don't really understand – not yet anyway," she replied. "Hopefully someday." Here was this humble young woman so far away from home who probably had sacrificed everything to serve her Heavenly Father. The Spirit was strong. My dad and I both began to weep.

We wished her well and left the center. We began the walk back up Main Street when my dad suddenly stopped. The thought came. The Spirit had spoken. He pulled out his wallet and emptied it into his hand. "Wait just a minute for me," he said, and ran back into the center. In a quiet corner he placed the money in her hand. She didn't want to take it. He explained that the Spirit had spoken to his heart and that he wanted to help support her mission expenses.

Dad returned to me on the street. I was crying – I knew what he was up to. He was crying. Another teaching moment for me. He said to me, "I've learned in my life that when the Spirit speaks I must respond immediately."

Sometimes we need comfort. Sometimes we need to be the one who provides the comfort. The Spirit is the communicator in both cases. What better investment can we make in our lives than to learn and practice receiving the message? It is a matter of priority. Find your space and open your heart. It is conversation at the highest level. A level where hope lives.

Chapter 7

The Strength of Burden

It was a typical hot summer day in the Arizona sun. The scout troop was excited and eager for the hike. This particular hike would test the endurance of the boys. The location – Havasu Canyon. About nine miles of hiking in the desert. My two brothers, Scott and Chad, were part of the troop along with my dad as one of the leaders. Everybody was in position at the trailhead with heavily loaded backpacks. Excitement was in the air. All members of the troop were gathered in a group listening to the guide. Suddenly the guide stopped and looked at my dad and said, "What's wrong with the boy?"

Chad had passed out and was lying on the ground white as a sheet. Dad knelt on the ground and worked on reviving him. As Chad opened his eyes, Dad began to wonder – "What do I do now? We are miles from home! Should I call my wife, meet her half way and then come back and do the trail later?" He suggested this to Chad.

In a small and weak voice Chad said, "If you can only carry my pack for a while, maybe I'll be okay." Dad wondered if the situation would get worse because they would be on the trail perhaps miles from the cars. Nevertheless, Dad tied Chad's pack to his own, took him by the hand and started down the trail. Chad was quiet and not very sure footed for a time. Soon he began to feel better and let go of Dad's hand. Finally, he looked up at Dad with eyes bright and color in his face. "Dad, I can take my pack now."

Perhaps all of us from time to time need to have someone carry our pack and equally important, we must be ready to carry another's pack. This is the message of the Savior.

"Come unto me, all ye that labour and are heavy laden, and I will give you rest" (Matthew 11:28).

A quick read of the Savior's words might suggest that if we are "heavy laden" or if we feel life's problems bearing down upon us, then a petition to Him may result in a lightening of our load. I think the reality of the meaning of the scripture lies not in a promise to lighten our load, but rather a promise to strengthen our back. That promise is central to the purpose of our journey here on Earth. A strong back earned as a result of enduring storms on difficult trails.[1]

When Helaman was teaching his sons he reminded them: *"That* **when** *the devil shall send forth his mighty winds, yea, his shafts in the whirlwind, yea when all his hail and his mighty storm shall beat upon you ... "* (Helaman 5:12).

Notice that it does not say "if" the devil shall send forth the mighty winds and storms, but "when." They will happen. It is one thing we can be sure of.

In seminary I used to teach the students this concept by comparing life to a bowl of cherries. Vibrant red – beautiful to look at – taste good. On the surface, life is beautiful and filled with joy and pleasure. Satan's plan was that life would always be good. He preferred the cherry pie filling. No pits. No work. No growth. We all understood a better Plan. We voted for Heavenly Father's Plan. We didn't just raise our hand to vote – we cheered for the chance to gain a body and live and experience it fully. Thus – life is like a bowl of cherries: it's all about the pits! Those pits are anything negative – sin, anger, death, hurt feelings, disappointments, etc. So we are going along through life – happy and carefree. Then one day you bite into a cherry and hit a pit. Satan wants you to say and feel that this "pit" in your life is too hard. That it's not fair. That God has deserted you.

He wants you to be as miserable and angry as he is. In fact it is his mission.

Think about those cherries – that red stain on your fingers from digging out those pits. Life is messy. There should be stains. That's the experience. Your greatest gift to God is who you become – with your stained fingers.

Rest in the Lord

Years ago we had the wonderful opportunity of hosting three different high school students in a foreign exchange program. They each lived with us for nine months and attended the high school in hopes of experiencing life in the United States and improving their English fluency. One was from Japan, another from Russia and our third from China. Although they each came from very different backgrounds and cultures, there was one common denominator. They each arrived in the United States expecting to speak and understand the English language upon arrival. All three had spent years studying our language in their schools. What they each learned within the first five minutes off the plane was that classroom English was very different from real conversations with real people. It was a rude and frightening introduction to a new reality of life.

Place yourself in their shoes for a moment. Imagine attending school in a foreign country where nobody speaks your language. Imagine chemistry in a foreign language – or biology or history. It was a true test of patience. They each had to go through the motions of attending class and soaking in whatever they could – knowing that eventually things would come together. It was a test of patience for us as a host family. Charades and hand gestures were a daily occurrence as my children desperately tried to help their new friends understand simple demands and questions. Family dynamics were altered and tested. It was difficult at times, but ultimately rewarding. What made the program a success for both the students and our family was patience. And lots of it.

Patience is the ability to put our desires on hold for a time. We want what we want immediately and right now. So the very idea of patience may seem unpleasant and bitter. But patience is precious and a rare virtue because so few people have it. It is something we should always be striving to improve. Yet few of us look forward to the opportunity to develop this painfully obtained quality. Without patience we cannot please God because it is a purifying process that refines understanding, deepens happiness, focuses action and offers hope for peace.

Patience presents the opportunity to be still and open. President Dieter F. Uchtdorf of the First Presidency teaches us that patience is not passive resignation or a failure to act because of our fears. Patience really means active waiting and enduring. It means staying with something and doing all that we can – working, hoping, and exercising faith. It means bearing hardship with fortitude, even when the desires of our hearts are delayed.

Impatience, however, is a symptom of selfishness. It describes one who is self-absorbed. Impatient people believe that the world revolves around them and that all others are just a supporting cast of characters in the grand theater of mortality in which only they have the starring role.

How many of us have been required to wait in our own way? We must wait for answers to prayers. We must wait for things which at the time appear so right and so good to us that we can't possibly imagine why Heavenly Father would delay the answer.[2]

In Doctrine and Covenants 24:8 the Lord tells us:

"Be patient in afflictions, for thou shalt have many; but endure them, for, lo, I am with thee, even unto the end of thy days."

There are many examples in the scriptures of this. In Alma 20:29 we learn about a band of missionaries who were *"patient in all their sufferings"* even though they were told before that there would be hardships. The principle taught is that trials are an opportunity to be a good example, to demonstrate inner strength and to learn how to endure to the very end.[3] The people of Alma were faithful despite life-threatening threats and persecutions yet *"they did submit cheerfully and with patience to all the will of the Lord"* (Mosiah 24:15). How steadfast they were! An example of great faith but also an example of patience in trusting the Lord in His timing.

How often do we waiver in our faith and lose our patience when faced with difficulties and trials? There are times when we or our loved ones encounter doubts which shake our testimonies. Doubts which begin as small cracks and fester into larger, deeper crevasses. Patience is continuing on even with those doubts. Patience is slowly and deliberately moving forward even with shaken beliefs in place, rather than tossing everything to the wind. Patience is recognizing and accepting that we don't have all the knowledge or understanding, yet still choosing to live and learn the gospel one day at a time. Patience is faith and hope in trusting His timing, not ours.

I marvel at the patience of my parents during this period of shingles. My mom has been a rock in daily medication monitoring and supporting Dad's need to frequently lie down and quiet the nerves. Her care for him has been patient and committed. In the beginning when the nerves were screaming at a horribly high level of pain, I used to call her about every day or so to cheer her on. "It should only be another week or so," we would say to each other. "Surely the nerves will quiet down next week." Weeks turned into months. Now months into years. The nerves still scream. Her belief that God is aware of the situation has never wavered.

Dad continues forward showing all who know him what patience looks like. When will this end? "It doesn't matter I suppose," he says. The anger at the situation is gone. His soul is healed as is everyone else's who lives this experience with him. His emotions are tender and his heart open as he lives each day to the fullest. A life of patience. A life of grace.

All of us struggle in this life. Some struggle with a vision and a purpose. They remember where they came from and where they are going. Others are not so fortunate. They struggle and are lost – they have lost the vision. We watch from a close distance with pained hearts. Each of us must go through the process. It seems natural to want to rescue them. Rescue our kids. Rescue our spouse. Rescue a friend. We want to lower the rope down to them and pull them out with all of our strength. But we need to visualize the ladder. They must climb out themselves. They learn patience in their own process of climbing up one step at a time. The process changes our hearts – softens them. First we must learn patience. Then we become teachable. Don't we want that for our children? For ourselves?

It doesn't mean that we can't hold the ladder steady – or shout words of encouragement from the top. "You can do this! I'm here for you!" We just can't climb the ladder for them or throw a rope down and pull them out ourselves. As much as we would like to rescue them, they must do it themselves. They must develop that beautiful virtue of patience. The fight that they find themselves in may rage ahead, but God will patiently wait to be welcomed in. I heard it once stated:

Sometimes God calms the storm …

Sometimes He lets the storm rage and calms His child

After a time I could see this change in my son. Austin's heart was open. He was patient. He was teachable. He welcomed God into his decisions and his soul. Once again he sang to the church congregation. Russian words flowed with conviction and testimony:

Be still, my soul: The Lord is on thy side
With patience bear thy cross of grief or pain
Leave to thy God to order and provide
In ev'ry change he faithful will remain

Be still, my soul: Thy best, thy heav'nly Friend
Thru thorny ways leads to a joyful end[4]

In the Old Testament we are told to *"Rest in the Lord, and wait patiently for Him"* (Psalms 37:7). Love that word "rest." Isn't that the blessing connected to applying patience? A better way of living. Patience is delaying immediate gratification for future blessings. It is accepting that which cannot be changed and facing it with courage, grace and faith. It is being firm and immovable in keeping the commandments of the Lord even when it is hard to do so. The Savior said that in your patience you possess your souls. It is knowing that sometimes it is in the waiting rather than the receiving that we grow the most. Truly it is a process of perfection.[5]

Endure It Well

I remember the first time I saw him. He wore white long sleeves and white long pants. His head was covered with a large white wide-brimmed hat with draping which hung down over the sides of his face and back of his neck. He was entirely protected from the hot sun on the hiking trail. He stood out from the rest. Unusual in appearance and initially unapproachable.

My curiosity was piqued. Who was he? I began to strike up simple conversations when I would see him on the trail. Our paths began to meet up at the top of Black Mountain trail which allowed more time. Conversations continued and I soon learned more about this man dressed in white. What a beautiful soul. A reverent spirit. A gentle and kind old man who was in his 80s. Still married to the first woman he ever fell in love with. Fostered over 20 children over the years and refers to them as "his kids." Currently battling prostate cancer. Weakened by the treatments, yet determined still to climb. Endurance for life. Still hiking his trails – one foot in front of the other.

I took notice and made a silent commitment. There were qualities in this fellow hiker that got my attention. I want his strong, silent endurance. I want to selflessly serve others. And I want to still be hiking the mountain well into my 80s.

Endure to the end. A common phrase heard often in lessons taught at church and throughout the scriptures. What does it really mean to endure? The definition given in the scriptures states:

"To remain firm in a commitment to be true to the commandments of God despite temptation, opposition, and adversity."[6]

Scriptures and statements from the prophets suggest that enduring is only the beginning. To endure it well – that is the goal.

"And then, if thou endure it well, God shall exalt thee on high; thou shalt triumph over all thy foes" (D&C 121:8).

Endure it well. What does that look like? I saw a young woman in the temple one day who I had spent some time counseling with months earlier about trials and suffering in her life. She was in spiritual and emotional pain over current situations in her family. It was a difficult hike. "I didn't sign up for this," she had cried earlier. Yet there she was in the temple. Head held high. Doing her part. Keeping and reminding herself of sacred covenants she had made despite life crumbling around her. Our eyes met. I walked over to her and wrapped my arms around her. I whispered in her ear. "You are a perfect example of not only enduring to the end, but enduring well." She was tearful, yet hopeful. That is what "enduring well" looks like.

There are so many others who have taught me what enduring it well looks like. It is similar to patience, yet has an added aspect of gospel commitment to it. Yes, my dad is incredibly patient in his suffering with shingles, but perhaps even more, he is enduring it well. He is determined not to be angry. That was a conscious choice. "God didn't cause this," he told me. "The church is still true." As he continues to allow others to serve him, he still looks for opportunities in his limited capacity to serve and bless those within his reach. That is what enduring it well looks like.

The test that a loving Heavenly Father has set before us is not to see if we can endure difficulty. It is to see if we can endure it well. We will pass the test by showing that we remembered Him and the commandments He gave us. To endure well is to keep those commandments whatever the opposition, whatever the temptation and whatever the tumult around us. We have a clear understanding because the restored gospel makes the Plan of Happiness so plain. Knowing why we are tested and what the real test is tells us how to get help. We must go to God. He has given us the commandments. And we will need much more than our own strength to keep them.[7]

My daughter Amber has two small children ages 3 and 2. Her husband is finishing his college degree and working full time. Life is good and she is blessed. But life has been challenging. The children have both had a myriad of medical conditions. There have been multiple hospital and doctor visits for testing, diagnostics and more testing, yet still there are many unresolved medical issues. Her life revolves around medical appointments, counseling sessions, physical therapists coming to the home, developmental preschool appointments – all while patiently trying to handle two darling but challenging little children.

There have been countless phone calls made from her front yard. Discouraging times when both kids have cried all day and Amber was seeking a moment of peace. Her patient and loving husband recognizes that look on her face on certain days when he walks in the door from work or school. "Go take a walk," he says. "I've got the kids." And so she calls me. It becomes a pep talk of sorts. We look for the silver lining of the day. It could be worse – we remind ourselves. Tomorrow is a new day.

One day she called me when the kids were napping after returning home from church. "I didn't hear a single thing said at church," she said. "Sometimes I wonder why I even go." But Amber still goes. She dresses the kids in their cutest clothes and combs their hair and heads to church each Sunday to juggle the kids and try to survive three of the most stressful hours of her week. And she goes because she knows it is where her family should be. She told me once, "Some days it's just simply obedience that gets me out the door to church. I can at least say that church was success- ful today because I was obedient."

In the evenings when long days have finally come to an end and her small children are finally put to bed, Amber pulls out her tablet. She learned about indexing. Countless entries of genealogical names and dates entered to support family history work for thousands of people who might be working on their own lines. In a challenging period of her life, Amber found a simple way to serve others for a few hours each week. A selfless service to those she will never meet. That is what enduring well looks like.

A passage of scripture that is most inspiring to me is Section 121 of the Doctrine and Covenants. The prophet Joseph Smith begins in the depths of despair and rises to celestial heights. We read that Joseph and a few of his followers were prisoners in the jail at Liberty, Missouri, from December 1838 until April 1839. "The jail had no heat and the food was barely edible. They were in a basement dungeon with a dirt floor and a ceiling so low they could not fully stand up. The Saints, meanwhile, had been driven from their homes. Amid this upheaval, Governor Lilburn W. Boggs issued his infamous extermination order."

Joseph asks, *"O God, where art thou? And where is the pavilion that covereth thy hiding place?"* (D&C 121:1) This is the same Joseph Smith who had heavenly visitations from God the Father, Jesus Christ, Moroni, John the Baptist, Peter, James, John and others. Shortly after his questions in the initial verses, Joseph expresses his frustration:

"Let thine anger be kindled against our enemies; and, in the fury of

thine heart, with thy sword avenge us of our wrongs. Remember thy suffering saints, O our God; and thy servants will rejoice in thy name forever" (D&C 121:5-6).

The Lord responds to Joseph's outpouring by saying, *"My son, peace be unto thy soul; thine adversity and thine afflictions shall be but a small moment"* (D&C 121:7).

Then He teaches Joseph a wonderful principle. *"And then, if thou endure it well, God shall exalt thee on high; thou shalt triumph over all thy foes"* (D&C 121:8).

The message is straightforward and succinct. We should not expect the Lord to remove our challenges just because we promise Him that we will always be faithful if He does. Rather, we are to endure it well, and then we will be blessed. That is a marvelous life lesson for each of us.

The greatest example we have of endurance is the life of the Savior. The Atonement required that He descend below all things and offer His perfect life on our behalf. In descending below all things, He suffered for all of life's misfortunes and sins, *"which suffering caused myself, even God, the greatest of all, to tremble because of pain, and to bleed at every pore, and to suffer both body and spirit"* (D&C 19:18).

Sometimes we forget that in premortality we fought alongside the Savior in defense of the Father's plan of moral agency. And we won! Lucifer and his followers were expelled, and we received the opportunity to experience the life we fought for. The Father's plan included the Atonement. Our job is to face our challenges and endure them well."[8] The Atonement of Jesus Christ is real and the promise is real that we can become new, changed and better. We can become stronger for the tests of life. In time we become His tested and strengthened disciples. A disciple of Christ – the power to become – because we have endured it well.

Surrender

We all want to be better – stronger – capable. Most of us pride ourselves on being self-sufficient. We strive for independence. Words like self-reliant and self-determination invoke positive and strong emotion. We desire to attain those qualities. It is a healthy and positive endeavor to work toward these goals.

Some of us (like me) are determined to succeed at "doing it myself." Somehow we feel better knowing that we were entirely able to accomplish the task or situation at hand without the help of anyone else. Pride enters and we truly believe that we know best and that our desires should prevail. Because it is our own life or the life of loved ones, surely we have an educated and informed opinion that commands attention. We have every intention to surrender to God's will as long as it agrees with ours. Persuasive prayers become the norm.

Words like "surrender" can sometimes have a negative connotation. It brings to mind situations such as withdraw, drop out, give up, back out, or fly the coop! But knowing God's will for us is perhaps the greatest important lesson we can learn in this life. And it involves surrendering to Him.

"For although a man may have many revelations, and have power to do many mighty works, yet if he boasts in his own strength, and sets at naught the counsels of God, and follows after the dictates of his own will and carnal desires, he must fall and incur the vengeance of a just God upon him" (D&C 3:4).

If we question everything we are asked to do, or dig in our heels at every unpleasant challenge, we make it harder for the Lord to bless us. The Lord is intent on our personal growth and development. That progress is accelerated when we willingly allow Him to lead us through every growth experience we encounter, whether initially it be to our individual liking or not. When we trust in the Lord and when we are willing to let our heart and our mind be centered in His will and when we ask to be led by the Spirit to do His will – we are assured of the greatest happiness along the way and the most fulfilling attainment from this mortal experience.[9]

"The submission of one's will is really the only uniquely personal thing we have to place on God's altar. The many other things we 'give,' ... are actually the things He has already given or loaned to us. However, when you and I finally submit ourselves, by letting our individual wills be swallowed up in God's will, then we are really giving something to Him! It is the only possession which is truly ours to give!"[10]

We have been commanded to *"be still, and know that I am God ... "* (Psalms 46:10). Some insight into the root meaning of these words provides clarity. This verse of scripture is not so much about meditation as it is about the mediation of God. The command to "be still" comes from the Hiphil stem of the verb "raphe," which means to be weak, to let go, or to release. This might better be translated as "cause yourself to let go" or "let yourselves become weak."

A quick Hebrew lesson is helpful. In Hebrew grammar, the emphasis of the coordinate commands "be still" and "know" is on the second requirement. In other words, we surrender in order to know that God is in control as the master of the universe. We must "let go" in order to objectively know the saving power of God in our lives. We actually give up trusting in ourselves and our own designs in order to experience the glory of God's fullness. When we surrender to the sure truth that God is in complete control of this world, we will find peace and be delivered from our temporal fears.[11]

It is having an eternal perspective. Heavenly Father has it – we should, too. It is living with hope. Hope fueled by faith allowing us to trust in the Lord enough to place our life in His hands. It is enabling us to say "Here it is, Heavenly Father – you know best. Thy will be done." He understands that we have lost our stamina on tough hikes. He's felt that. But He also knows the end. He's hiked this trail before and He knows what it can do for us – for our children – for our future. And so we allow Him to lead because we know that He also knows the end.

How beautifully descriptive the words to the second verse of "Be Still My Soul:"

Be still, my soul: Thy God doth undertake
To guide the future as he has the past.
Thy hope, thy confidence let nothing shake;
All now mysterious shall be bright at last.[12]

On the most difficult hiking trails in life, we must do all that we can. It is having faith that He is the architect of our hike. He knows our thoughts, our heart and our desires. But he also knows the terrain, the dangers and the difficulties. Pray from the heart and soul. Sacrifice time and talents. Learn the doctrine. Commune with the Spirit. Trust that the Lord knows best. My will be Thy will. Take a deep breath – and surrender.

Chapter 8

Hope – an Anchor to the Soul

The sun was high in the sky and the temperature was hot. Not unusual for the Arizona desert. Today the cross country race would be difficult. The heat would play a role. My sister Gretchen was on the high school team and ready to run. This 3-mile course was a particularly tough course because toward the end of the race there was a huge hill at Papago Park that was very steep and discouraged many runners.

Much to Gretchen's dismay, my dad was at every meet. During this time of her life she was an "independent soul." I suppose she was a teenager striving for some autonomy and she sometimes felt his love and support just wasn't cool. They announced the start of the race and the runners approached. Gretchen was ready and took her place at the starting line. A quick look to the crowd. She did not see Dad.

And the runners were off! All the kids took off – running up and down the trails and through the desert terrain. When Dad arrived at the race and did a quick survey of the course, he knew the real difficulty lie in that final hill. So he quickly circled back around and ran to the top of that hill to cheer for Gretchen.

The runners were really feeling the heat now. The high temperature was having an effect on everyone. By the time they reached that last hill, they were out of steam. Dad watched from the top of the hill as runners gave up at the bottom and began walking the hill – too tired to continue their pace. He waited and watched.

Gretchen ran the last turn before the hill. She was hot and tired. She looked up at the hill. It was too much. She gave up and began to walk. Then she heard a whistle. That distinctive shrill whistle. Dad's whistle. Gretchen pulled her head up and looked at the top of the hill. There he was. Cheering her on. Words of encouragement. Dad knew she could do it. And she believed him. Gretchen started to run. With everything she had she ran to the top of that hill with tears streaming down her face. She finished the race and ran over to find Dad who was also crying now. A tender moment for them both.

I suppose that Heavenly Father feels the same way when He looks down at us in our struggles. He is at the top of the hill cheering us on and feels great emotion at our pain and despair in continuing the race. He knows that we are tired. But He also sees the end.

"For I know the thoughts that I think toward you, saith the Lord, thoughts of peace, and not of evil, to give you an expected end" (Jeremiah 29:11).

And so we continue to run. We must conquer the mountain. God will not move the mountain, but He will help us climb. One race at a time.

Your "Liberty Jail"

Each of us can have a sacred, revelatory, profoundly instructive experience with the Lord in any situation that we are in. Even in the most miserable experiences of our lives – in the worst settings, while enduring the most painful injustices and when facing the most insurmountable odds and opposition that we have ever faced.

In one way or another – great or small – every one of us is going to spend a little time in Liberty Jail – spiritually speaking. We may face things that may not be our fault. We may face difficult circumstances for reasons that were absolutely right and proper – because we were trying to keep the commandments of the Lord. We may face persecution. We may endure heartache and separation from loved ones. We may be cold and hungry. We may be given a little taste of what the prophets faced often in their lives.

The truths that Joseph Smith received while in Liberty Jail reveal that God was not only teaching him in that small, dirty prison, but He was also teaching all of us for generations yet to come. One lesson from Liberty Jail is that everyone – including and perhaps especially the righteous – will be called upon to face trying times. We sometimes succumb to the fear that God has abandoned us or that He does not hear our prayers. We must turn that fear over to faith that He does hear and see and love us. We are not alone in our little prison. When suffering we may actually be nearer to God than we have ever been in our entire lives. The Lord, in his everlasting declaration of love for us has promised:

"I will go before your face. I will be on your right hand and on your left, and my Spirit shall be in your hearts, and mine angels round about you, to bear you up" (D&C 84:88).

A second lesson learned is just because difficult things happen does not mean that we are unrighteous or unworthy of blessings, or that God is disappointed in us. Let us remember that the same thing had happened to the Savior. Not only did He suffer, but so have most of the prophets and other great men and women recorded in the scriptures. If you are having a bad day, you have lots of very good company.

Finally, we must remember that even when we face distressing circumstances in our life and there is something in us that wants to strike out at God or man or friend, we must remember that *"no power or influence can or ought to be maintained ... except by persuasion, by long-suffering, by gentleness and meekness, and by love unfeigned ... without hypocrisy and without guile"* (D&C 121:41-42). The real test of our faith and of our Christian discipleship is when things are not going smoothly. This is when we get to see what we are made of and how strong our commitment to the gospel really is. Remaining true is the only way that divine influence can help us. The Spirit has a very difficult, if not impossible task to get through to a heart that is filled with hate or anger or vengeance or self-pity. On the other hand, the Spirit finds instant access to a heart striving to be charitable and forgiving, long-suffering and kind.[1]

Within our own "Liberty Jail" experience, we must find the strength to rise above our circumstances. An eternal perspective at this time is critical. Once again, Elder Jeffrey R. Holland challenges us:

"May we declare ourselves to be more fully disciples of the Lord Jesus Christ, not in word only and not only in the flush of comfortable times but in deed and in courage and in faith, including when the path is lonely and when our cross is difficult to bear."[2]

Here is Hope

Hope is defined as *"the confident expectation of and longing for the promised blessings of righteousness."*[3] We desperately look for it. It comes from our belief in God and His goodness and creates an anchor in our soul.

"Wherefore, whoso believeth in God might with surety hope for a better world, yea, even a place at the right hand of God, which hope cometh of faith, maketh an anchor to the souls of men, which would make them sure and steadfast, always abounding in good works, being led to glorify God" (Ether 12:4).

This anchor of hope is the silver lining. It is delivered to our senses through the Holy Ghost during difficult times:

"And because of meekness and lowliness of heart cometh the visitation of the Holy Ghost, which Comforter filleth with hope and perfect love ... " (Moroni 8:26).

It is a belief of better things. It is a destination – a place we want to be. And it is given to us in small glimpses. It is enough to enable us to carry on. To take one more step. To try again. And to understand the promise.

"Wherefore, ye must press forward with a steadfastness in Christ, having a perfect brightness of hope, and a love of God and of all men. Wherefore, if ye shall press forward, feasting upon the word of Christ, and endure to the end, behold, thus saith the Father: Ye shall have eternal life" (2 Nephi 31:20).

Hope is not only a destination or a desired state or place. Hope is also a verb. Something that we strive to do. We declare it in the 13th Article of Faith:

"We believe in being honest, true, chaste, benevolent, virtuous, and in doing good to all men; indeed, we may say that we follow the admonition of Paul – We believe all things, we hope all things, we have endured many things, and hope to be able to endure all things. If there is anything virtuous, lovely, or of good report or praiseworthy, we seek after these things."

To hope for is a process – a process that takes some real work. The goal is to reach into our soul with every fiber of our testimony and to move forward with purpose. It is trusting God. And it is turning our will over to Him believing and yearning for that ultimate promise of eternal life. As we anchor ourselves to hope, we take the focus off ourselves and put that focus on Christ. If we are looking toward the light of Christ, then we are filled with light – even if we don't see it at the time.

"You and I in a moment of weakness may cry out, 'No one understands. No one knows.' No human being, perhaps, knows. But the Son of God perfectly knows and understands for He felt and bore our burdens before we ever did."[4] The scriptures teach that this process of hope is connected to the Atonement:

"And what is it that ye shall hope for? Behold I say unto you that ye shall have hope through the atonement of Christ and the power of his resurrection, to be raised unto life eternal, and this because of your faith in him according to

the promise" (Moroni 7:41).

Think about who you are becoming. All the tough hikes in your life have formed you. We continue to be a work in progress. Those which are most difficult really shape us and cause us to reach up and grasp the Lord's hand. He is always there waiting – waiting to pick us up and dust us off. But we must reach for Him.

His Atonement provides hope for each of us and all our bumps and scrapes and cracks. The chorus of Leonard Cohen's song "Anthem" says:

Ring the bells that still can ring
Forget your perfect offering
There is a crack in everything
That's how the light gets in.

Our bells are cracked. Perfection is not possible in this life. We must hope for and embrace the healing power of the Atonement which brings us closer to Christ. This healing power of Christ comes in through our cracks and imperfections. The hope is in the healing and in the promise of who we will become.

Hope originates in Christ's sacrifice for us. The victory of hope is ours as we contemplate and understand the role of the Atonement in our life. The lyrics to a beautiful song entitled, "Here is Hope" express it well:

He who healed our sorrows
Here was bruised and broken
He whose love no end knows
Here was forsaken, Left all alone.

Here despair cries boldly
Claiming this its victory

Sweeter peace enfolds me
Hope did not die here, But here was given.

Here is Hope.

He who was rejected
He knows well my longing
He, so long expected
Carried our burdens, Bore every sorrow.

Here is Hope.

Hope did not die here
But here was given
And ours is the victory.

Here is Hope.[5]

Color To My Sunset

"Clouds come floating into my life, no longer to carry rain or usher storm, but to add color to my sunset sky."[6]

It is what we choose to see. Hope can be felt. Hope can be seen. Hope can be heard. But our senses have to be keen to it. We must have an understanding of His Plan and be actively looking for it. Spirit and soul wide open to receive.

My daughter Aubreigh pulled up in the driveway to our home and reached up to turn off the ignition. Her clothes and belongings were boxed up in the back seat of the car. She couldn't move. And she began to cry. Her first marriage was ending after just one short year. She thought she had life figured out. Married in the temple. Kept her covenants. Nothing was as it had seemed. Where were the blessings? She sat in the driveway – unable to move for a long time. To move back into her childhood bedroom made this real. A sign of defeat.

And so she began to pray. Not any prayer like she had ever uttered before. A prayer from her heart and soul begging for comfort. For courage to move forward. She promised her commitment to the gospel in exchange. "Please … let me know you are there … let me know love."

Aubreigh wiped her tears and climbed out of the car. She silently made her way back to the familiar bedroom. She threw herself on the bed. There was something on her pillow. A little white envelope tied up with a red string. Earlier that evening her little 10-year-old sister Ashlyn had thought to write her older sister a note:

"Do NOT open this envelope. Inside is a kiss and a hug from me to you! When it opens, all will float away and nothing will be left so keep it safe and shut! When you need a kiss and hug, hold the envelope and I will be with you. Love, Ashlyn."

It was a tender mercy. It was hope at the lowest point in her life. Aubreigh knew that God loved her and knew of her despair. She did not know what the future would hold, but she felt hope and trusted that someday she would smile again. And she did. A new loving husband and two darling boys give her plenty of reason. She keeps the little white envelope with the red string in her scriptures. It is a daily reminder of her commitment to the gospel and her relationship with Heavenly Father. It is a reminder of hope.

Hope can take the form of many things. It is up to us to recognize it for what it is. John McCain was a prisoner of war in Vietnam. In prison his captors would tie his arms behind his back and then loop the rope around his neck and ankles so that his head was pulled down between his knees. He was often left like that throughout the night. One night a guard came into his cell. He put his finger to his lips signaling for John to be quiet and then loosened his ropes to relieve the pain. The next morning, when his shift ended, the guard returned and retightened the ropes, never saying a word to him.

A month or so later, on Christmas Day, John was standing in the dirt courtyard when he saw that same guard approach him. He walked up and stood silently next to John, not looking or smiling at him. Then he used his sandaled foot to draw a cross in the dirt. They stood wordlessly looking at the cross, remembering the true light of Christmas – even in the darkness of a Vietnamese prison camp.

The message of hope can reach into any place, however dark. Even in solitary confinement, when everything else has been taken away, nothing can separate us from the love of our Creator.[7]

Elder Bednar reminds us:

"We should not underestimate or overlook the power of the Lord's tender mercies. The simpleness, the sweetness, and the constancy of the tender mercies of the Lord will do much to fortify and protect us in the troubled times in which we do now and will yet live. When words cannot provide the solace we need or express the joy we feel, when it is simply futile to attempt to explain that which is unexplainable, when logic and reason cannot yield adequate understanding about the injustices and inequities of life, when mortal experience and evaluation are insufficient to produce a desired outcome, and when it seems that perhaps we are so totally alone, truly we are blessed by the tender mercies of the Lord and made mighty even unto the power of deliverance."[8]

Austin woke to the sound of rain. It had been a long night. Bad dreams, a failed relationship and a broken heart had kept him up most of the night. His confidence was beaten and he felt defeated. He and I had talked for some time weeks before. Together on the phone we talked about life's ups and downs. I reminded Austin of his good, tender heart. Of his desire to live a righteous life and eventually take a sweetheart to the temple to be sealed for eternity. His priorities were set. Reading the scriptures daily. Serving others and exercising to keep those endorphins pumping.

But the rain. Again. He had not been able to climb or run or bike for days because of the endless rain. He dropped to his knees next to his bed and began to pray. "Please Heavenly Father – I need a break. I can't do this." He offered up his soul.

Suddenly the rain stopped. He listened for the drops on the window. Silence. He looked outside. Dark black clouds were thick – but a break in the moisture. A tender mercy. An incredible answer to his prayer. He recognized it. He knew without a doubt.

So Austin jumped on his bike to head for the mountain trail. All around him the dark clouds moved in – threatening to burst into a storm. He powered up the trail uttering prayers of gratitude for this small miracle. A simple space of time. A space where he could move his muscles and clear his mind. A space to open up his heart and soul. To feel.

Part way up the mountain he saw a thicket of flowers. Beautiful yellow flowers. It was a breathtaking sight. He stopped on the trail, and jumped off the bike to walk a few steps over and take it all in. Grateful for the peace it seemed to represent. He turned back toward his bike. And there it was. A single yellow flower perfectly positioned in the center of his handlebars. How did it get there? He was alone on the trail. He had only walked away for a minute. And suddenly he knew. A tender sign of hope. He felt it in his soul. A message from God. It was going to be okay.

Austin took a picture on his cellphone of the flower and texted it to me, "A message of hope for me." I immediately called him. He was emotional as he told me the story. His heart was full. My heart was full. I knew that his heart was in a spiritual position to have recognized the message. We cried together. Two hearts full of hope for the future. Certain that God lives. Ready to move forward.

Photograph by Austin Tucker

Climb Your Mountain

The older I get, the more I do not believe in coincidence. It is defined as "a striking occurrence of two or more events at one time apparently by mere chance."[9] I would venture to say that there are no coincidences in life – only those who do not see the spiritual connections. It takes some training and effort on our part for our spirit to notice them. It allows us to see our life as God would see it.

Believing you can is key. Erik Weihenmayer was the first blind climber to scale Mt. Everest. He still climbs 50 days a year. He was asked what he looks for in teammates. He says, "I look for people who have an unrealistic optimism about life. I hear people say, 'Seeing is believing.' I want people who believe the opposite, 'Believing is seeing.' You've got to believe first in what you're doing and be sure you have a reason to believe it."[10]

One day I was sitting at the top of Black Mountain pondering my blessings and considering the beauty of the desert around me. A random thought came out of nowhere and spoke firmly to my mind. "I gave you depression so you would know me." It shook me. The truth of it sunk deep. I froze for several minutes as moments of my life flashed before me in a continuum that bound them all together in one purpose. Because of depression I had to make a practice of finding peace and stillness in my mind. The mountain is the best place for me to find that space. To find that channel. Who knew that one of the greatest trials in my life would lead to a process which would become the greatest gift in forming and molding my exchanges and relationship with Heavenly Father? Who needs adversity? We all do! Adversity well-handled is really a blessing in disguise.

When in the midst of those really difficult hikes, we sometimes forget the basics. Life is spinning so out of control that we lose ourselves for a bit. Everything mortal screams with selfish reasoning. We want to protect ourselves. Hunker down. Pull inward. Prayers initially become an afterthought. Scriptures build up some dust and serving others is out of the question. What about me? It is natural to attend our own "pity party" for some time, but our spirit knows better. Our spirit anticipates the experience. It knows that it is a sure process to growth and strength.

And so we need to pick ourselves up and pull those tools out of our backpacks and put them to use. Tools and patterns discussed in this book that will bring our focus from our sorrows to Him. Let us remember that the journey of thousands of miles always begins with a single step. Whatever the challenge we can face it one step at a time. The Lord didn't do it all in one day. What makes me think I can?

Around Cave Creek each May I often see people on hiking trails wearing backpacks loaded with rocks or steel weights. They are training their bodies for the ultimate Arizona hike – the Grand Canyon. Endurance is essential. Why not prepare ourselves and build some endurance in ourselves for future trials? It is conditioning your spirit. It is so important to condition our spirit because it is not a matter of IF you will encounter a difficult hike in your life, but WHEN. A conditioned spirit is open to heavenly communication. A conditioned spirit knows a tender mercy. And a conditioned spirit recognizes hope.

Find Your Stories

I have always wanted to be a teacher. To teach from what I know. To share with others who are hurting, weeping, distraught, bewildered and weary of the battle. I have told my stories. You have stories, too. The details are different, but we all share the spiritual messages. And we all share pain.

And so we fight the battles. Battles which wear us down and exhaust us physically, mentally, spiritually. We were meant to battle. It is what makes us learn and grow to be more like Him. It is why we are here. But we are not abandoned. There is hope. Glimpses of hope that are unique and divinely meant just for you. We must watch and listen and tune all senses. It is positioning your heart, mind and soul to recognize the messages of hope from God. They are there. And they come in many forms – a phone call, a scripture, a friend, a voice, butterflies, sunbeams through the clouds, a song, a note on your pillow, a yellow flower, a moment on the mountain. It is putting yourself in a position to receive your spiritual message. A message which will carry you forward.

Put yourself in position by praying diligently and specifically for your heart's desires. Don't just read the scriptures – search them. Devour them. They are the voice of the Lord. Serve despite your challenges. Remember and honor the memory and legacy of those family members who went before you. Your dedication and example will honor them and be a lighthouse for your own children. Learn and practice a higher level of communication with the Spirit. It will comfort and guide you as you not just endure difficulties – but endure them well. And lift your head up as you surrender your will to His. It is totally trusting Him. Trusting that you are exactly where you should be.

Some say life gets in the way. No – life is the way. It is taking what is thrown at you and then finding those spiritual hiking tools to continue on your own personal path up the rocky ridge. The tools are key because they are the impetus to finding hope.

Hope is that gust of wind against our back. A pat on the back. Rewarded belief. A thumbs up from God. A cool breeze on a hot summer day. Hope is confidence.

What's next? I'm not sure. There are lots of trails ahead. Beautiful rolling trails lined with wildflowers. Moderate trails to test my endurance. Rocky ridges and steep inclines to battle through. It's okay. I've got my tools. I know my Guide.

See you on the mountain.

"Being challenged in life is mandatory. Being defeated is optional."

Robert Crawford

Tell me about your story of hope. I may include it in my next book.
Visit my website: **www.thepickledsunflower.com**

About the Author

Heidi Tucker was born and raised in the beautiful desert of Arizona. Following her graduation from Arizona State University she raised her family and found a strong connection working with the youth. Her favorite getaway is a good long hike in the mountainous regions of Arizona and Utah. Her passion for hiking paves the way for quiet reflection of life's journey and compliments an eagerness to write and speak about it. When she's not at the top of a mountain solving life's problems, you'll find her with friends and family at the bottom of the ocean scuba diving. Between Mount Timpanogos and the Caribbean Ocean, Heidi will always find a way to tell a story and teach a principle.

For more book updates and weekly writings about light and hope, visit Heidi Tucker at **www.thepickledsunflower.com**

NOTES

Chapter 1 – I Am a Child of God

[1] Hartman Rector Jr., Conference Report, Apr. 1970, p. 101-2.

[2] Naomi W. Randall, "I Am A Child of God," in Hymns of The Church of Jesus Christ of Latter-day Saints (Salt Lake City: The Church of Jesus Christ of Latter-day Saints, 1985), no. 301.

Chapter 2 – Seek Me Diligently

[1] "Prayer," Bible Dictionary.

[2] Clark Cederlof, "Prayer," Gospel Reflections.

[3] Teachings of Presidents of the Church: Lorenzo Snow, 2011.

[4] James Montgomery, "Prayer Is the Soul's Sincere Desire," in Hymns of The Church of Jesus Christ of Latter-day Saints (Salt Lake City: The Church of Jesus Christ of Latter-day Saints, 1985), no. 145.

[5] "Prayer," Bible Dictionary.

[6] "Abide," Dictionary.com.

[7] Gordon B. Hinckley, "The Fabric of Faith and Testimony," Ensign, November 1995.

[8] David A. Bednar, "Pray Always," Ensign, November 2008.

[9] D. Todd Christofferson, "How Can I Make Daily Prayer More Meaningful?" Ensign October 2010.

[10] Gospeldoctrine.com: Alma 32:10.

[11] Joseph B. Wirthlin, "Finding Peace in Our Lives, p. 163.

[12] Gospeldoctrine.com: Alma 34:26.

[13] Clark Cederlof, "Prayer," Gospel Reflections.

[14] Colorado Springs Young Adult Meeting, April 14, 1996 as taken from the Teachings of Gordon B. Hinckley.

[15] "Diligently," Dictionary.com.

[16] D. Todd Christofferson, "How Can I Make Daily Prayer More Meaningful?" Ensign October 2010.

[17] Charles D. Tillman, "Unanswered Yet," pub. 1883.

[18] Alice D. Domar, PhD, "Be Happy Without Being Perfect: How to Worry Less and Enjoy Life More."

[19] Clark Cederlof, "Return Our Thanks To God," Gospel Reflections.

Chapter 3 – His Hands. His Voice. His Hug.

[1] Neal A. Maxwell, "If Thou Endure It Well", p. 94.

[2] Joseph B. Wirthlin, "The Virtue of Kindness," General Conference, April 2005.

[3] Eze, M.O. Intellectual History in Contemporary South Africa, pp. 190-191.

[4] Robert J. Whetten, "Strengthen Thy Brethren," General Conference, April 2005.

[5] "Goodness," Dictionary.com.

[6] James Talmage, Articles of Faith.

[7] Brent Cederlof, "History of Lucille Genet Murphy Cederlof."

[8] Robert D. Hales, "Welfare Principles to Guide Our Lives: An Eternal Plan for the Welfare of Men's Souls," Ensign, May 1986.

[9] Derek A. Cuthbert, "The Spirituality of Service," General Conference, April 1990.

[10] Dieter F. Uchtdorf, "You Are My Hands" General Conference, April 2010.

[11] Richard G. Scott, "Why Every Member a Missionary" General Conference, November 1997.

[12] Jeffrey R. Holland, "Israel, Israel, God Is Calling" CES Devotional May 2012.

[13] Jeffrey R. Holland, "None Were With Him," General Conference, April 2009.

Chapter 4 – Words of Direction

[1] Teachings of Harold B. Lee, 450-51.

[2] Joseph B. Wirthlin, "Living Water to Quench Spiritual Thirst," General Conference, April 1995.

[3] "Scripture Power," The Friend, Copyright © 1987 by Clive Romney.

[4] Jeffrey R. Holland, "Christ and the New Covenant" p. 9.

[5] "Explanatory Introduction" The Doctrine and Covenants.

[6] Gospeldoctrine.com: 2 Nephi 32:3.

[7] "Ponder" Dictionary.com.

[8] Clark Cederlof, "Search, Ponder, and Pray," Gospel Reflections.

[9] Bruce R. McConkie, Doctrinal New Testament Commentary, 3 vols., Salt Lake City: Bookcraft, 1965–73, 1:762.

Chapter 5 – True to the Faith

[1] Brad Wilcox, "The Continuous Conversion" p 143-145.

[2] William R. Walker, "Live True to the Faith" General Conference, April 2014.

[3] History of Pleasant Green Taylor.

[4] Breck England, "The Life and Thought of Orson Pratt," University of Utah Press 1985.

[5] A. Philip Cederlof, "A Sketch of the Life of Mary Bjork Cederlof," 1951.

[6] Clark Cederlof, "Pioneer Spirit," Gospel Reflections.

[7] Teachings of the Prophet Joseph Smith, p. 326.

[8] "There Are Angels" text and music by Rob Gardner.

[9] Joseph F. Smith, "Gospel Doctrine," Salt Lake City: Deseret Book Co., 1970, pages 435-36.
[10] Teachings of Harold B. Lee, p. 58.
[11] Jeffrey R. Holland, "For Times of Trouble," BYU Devotional, March 1980.

Chapter 6 – Messenger of Hope

[1] Parley P. Pratt, "Key to the Science of Theology, 9th ed. Salt Lake City: Deseret Book Co. 1965, p. 101.
[2] Church News Viewpoint, "Oft Overlooked," December 2, 2006.
[3] Boyd K. Packer, "How Does the Spirit Speak to Us" New Era, February 2010.
[4] Kristine Carlson, "Don't Sweat the Small Stuff for Women," 2001.
[5] M. Russell Ballard, "Be Still, and Know That I Am God," CES Devotional for Young Adults, May 2014.
[6] Erin D. Maughan, "Be Still, and Know God," BYU Speech August 4, 2009.
[7] Michelle Marchant, "My Life Is a Gift; My Life Has a Plan," BYU Speech April 2, 2013.
[8] Richard G. Scott, "To Acquire Spiritual Guidance," General Conference October 2009.
[9] Boyd K. Packer, "Prayer and Promptings," General Conference, October 2009.
[10] F. Enzio Busche, "University for Eternal Life," General Conference, April 1989.
[11] David B. Haight, "Temples and Work Therein," Ensign, November 1990, p 61.
[12] Gordon B. Hinckley, Fireside. Taipei, Taiwan, May 23 1996.
[13] Author unknown, "Temple Attendance Blessings."
[14] M. Russell Ballard, "Be Still, and Know That I Am God," CES Devotional for Young Adults, May 2014.
[15] Thomas S. Monson, "A Refuge from the Storms of Life," Church News, March 9, 2014, 5.
[16] J.K. Rowling, Harry Potter: Albus Dumbledore Quotes.
[17] Kurt Bestor, "Prayer of the Children," wrote words and music.
[18] Marvin J. Ashton, "The Time Is Now," General Conference, April 1975.

Chapter 7 – The Strength of Burden

[1] Clark Cederlof, "The Strength of Burden," Gospel Reflections.
[2] Dieter F. Uchtdorf, "Continue in Patience," Ensign, May 2010.
[3] Gospel Doctrine.com: Alma 20:29.
[4] Katharina von Schlegel, "Be Still My Soul," in Hymns of The Church of Jesus Christ of Latter-day Saints (Salt Lake City: The Church of Jesus Christ of Latter-day Saints, 1985), no. 124.
[5] Dieter F. Uchtdorf, "Continue in Patience." Ensign, May 2010.
[6] The Guide to the Scriptures: Endure.
[7] Henry B. Eyring, "In the Strength of the Lord," General Conference, April 2004.
[8] J. Christopher Lansing, "Enduring Well," Devotional Address October 30, 2012.

[9] Richard G. Scott, "Finding Joy in Life," General Conference, April 1996.

[10] Neal A. Maxwell, "Swallowed Up in the Will of the Father," General Conference, October 1995.

[11] John J. Parsons, "Surrender…God's Irrepressible Care of the World," Hebrew4christians. com.

[12] Katharina von Schlegel, "Be Still My Soul," in Hymns of The Church of Jesus Christ of Latter-day Saints (Salt Lake City: The Church of Jesus Christ of Latter-day Saints, 1985), no. 124.

Chapter 8 – Hope – an Anchor to the Soul

[1] Jeffrey R. Holland, "Lessons from Liberty Jail," CES Fireside, September 7, 2008.

[2] Jeffrey R. Holland, "None Were With Him," General Conference, April 2009.

[3] The Guide to the Scriptures: Hope.

[4] David A. Bednar, "The Atonement and the Journey of Mortality," General Conference April 2012.

[5] Rob Gardner Music 2012, "Here is Hope."

[6] Rabindranath Tagore, "Stray Birds."

[7] John McCain, "A Light Amid the Darkness," Time Magazine, August 18, 2008.

[8] David A. Bednar, "The Tender Mercies of the Lord," General Conference, April 2005.

[9] "Coincidence," Dictionary.com.

[10] Danielle Sacks, "60 Seconds With Erik Weihenmayer," Fast Company magazine May 2004.

BIBLIOGRAPHY

A. Philip Cederlof, "A Sketch of the Life of Mary Bjork Cederlof." 1951.

Ashton, Marvin J., "The Time Is Now." General Conference April 1975.

Author unknown, "Temple Attendance Blessings."

Ballard, M. Russell, "Be Still, and Know That I Am God." CES Devotional for Young Adults. May 2014.

Bednar, David A., "Pray Always." Ensign. November 2008.

Bednar, David A., "The Atonement and the Journey of Mortality." General Conference. April 2012.

Bednar, David A., "The Tender Mercies of the Lord," General Conference, April 2005.

Bestor, Kurt, "Prayer of the Children." Words and music 1997.

Bible Dictionary, "Prayer."

Busche, F. Enzio, "University for Eternal Life." General Conference. April 1989.

Carlson, Kristine, Don't Sweat the Small Stuff for Women. New York: Hyperion 2001.

Cederlof, Brent, History of Lucille Genet Murphy Cederlof. October 1995.

Cederlof, Clark, Gospel Reflections. "Pioneer Spirit." 2000.

Cederlof, Clark, Gospel Reflections. "Prayer." 2000.

Cederlof, Clark, Gospel Reflections. "Return Our Thanks To God." 2000.

Cederlof, Clark, Gospel Reflections. "Search, Ponder, and Pray," 2000.

Cederlof, Clark, Gospel Reflections. "The Strength of Burden," 2000.

Cederlof, Clark, History of Pleasant Green Taylor. Interview.

Christofferson, D. Todd, "How Can I Make Daily Prayer More Meaningful?" Ensign. October 2010.

Church News Viewpoint, "Oft Overlooked." December 2, 2006.

Cuthbert, Derek A., "The Spirituality of Service." General Conference. April 1990.

Dictionary.com. Abide. (Online).

Dictionary.com. Coincidence. (Online).

Dictionary.com. Diligently. (Online).

Dictionary.com. Goodness. (Online)

Dictionary.com. Ponder. (Online)

Domar, Alice D. PhD. Be Happy Without Being Perfect: How to Worry Less and Enjoy Life More. New York City: Three Rivers Press 2008.

England, Breck, The Life and Thought of Orson Pratt. University of Utah Press 1981.

Eyring, Henry B., "In the Strength of the Lord." General Conference. April 2004.

Eze, Michael Onyebuchi, Intellectual History in Contemporary South Africa. New York City: Palgrave MacMillan 2010.

Gardner, Rob, "Here Is Hope." Words and music 2012.

Gardner, Rob, "There Are Angels." Words and music. 2012.

Gospeldoctrine.com. Bryan Richards. 2 Nephi 32:3.

Gospeldoctrine.com. Bryan Richards. Alma 20:29.

Gospeldoctrine.com. Bryan Richards. Alma 32:10.

Gospeldoctrine.com. Bryan Richards. Alma 34:26.

Haight, David B., "Temples and Work Therein." Ensign. November 1990.

Hales, Robert D., "Welfare Principles to Guide Our Lives: An Eternal Plan for the Welfare Of Men's Souls." Ensign. May 1986.

Hinckley, Gordon B., "The Fabric of Faith and Testimony." Ensign. November 1995.

Hinckley, Gordon B., Fireside. Taipei, Taiwan. May 23, 1996.

Hinckley, Gordon B., Teachings of Gordon B. Hinckley. Colorado Springs Young Adult Meeting, April 14, 1996.

Holland, Jeffrey R., "For Times of Trouble." BYU Devotional. March 1980.

Holland, Jeffrey R., "Israel, Israel, God Is Calling." CES Devotional. May 2012.

Holland, Jeffrey R., "Lessons from Liberty Jail.'CES Fireside. September 7, 2008.

Holland, Jeffrey R., "None Were With Him." General Conference. April 2009.

Holland, Jeffrey R., Christ and the New Covenant. Salt Lake City: Deseret Book 1997.

Lansing, J. Christopher, "Enduring Well." Devotional Address. October 30, 2012.

LDS.org. "The Guide to the Scriptures." Endure. (Online)

LDS.org. "The Guide to the Scriptures." Hope. (Online)

Lee, Harold B., Teachings of Harold B. Lee. Salt Lake City: Bookcraft 1996.

Marchant, Michelle, "My Life Is a Gift; My Life Has a Plan." BYU Speech. April 2, 2013.

Maughan, Erin D., "Be Still, and Know God." BYU Speech. August 4, 2009.

Maxwell, Neal A., "Swallowed Up in the Will of the Father." General Conference. October 1995.

Maxwell, Neal A., If Thou Endure It Well. Salt Lake City: Bookcraft 1996.

McCain, John, "A Light Amid the Darkness." Time Magazine. August 18, 2008.

McConkie, Bruce R., Doctrinal New Testament Commentary. 3 vols., Salt Lake City: Bookcraft 1965-73.

Monson, Thomas S., "A Refuge from the Storms of Life." Church News. March 9, 2014.

Montgomery, James, "Prayer Is the Soul's Sincere Desire." Hymns of The Church ofJesus Christ of Latter-day Saints. Salt Lake City: The Church of Jesus Christ of Latter-day Saints 1985.

Packer, Boyd K., "How Does the Spirit Speak to Us?" New Era. February 2010.

Packer, Boyd K., "Prayer and Promptings." General Conference. October 2009.

Parsons, John J., "Surrender...God's Irrepressible Care of the World."

Hebrew4christians.com.

Pratt, Parley P., Key to the Science of Theology. 9th edition. Salt Lake City: DeseretBook 1965.

Randall, Naomi W., "I Am A Child of God." Hymns of The Church of Jesus Christ of Latter-day Saints. Salt Lake City: The Church of Jesus Christ of Latter-day Saints 1985.

Rector, Hartman Jr., Conference Report. April 1970.

Romney, Clive, "Scripture Power." The Friend. October 1987.

Rowling, J. K., Harry Potter: Albus Dumbledore Quotes. (Online)

Sacks, Danielle, "60 Seconds With Erik Weihenmayer." Fast Company. May 2004.

Scott, Richard G., "Finding Joy in Life." General Conference. April 1996.

Scott, Richard G., "To Acquire Spiritual Guidance." General Conference. October 2009.

Scott, Richard G., "Why Every Member a Missionary?" General Conference. November 1997.

Smith, Joseph F., Gospel Doctrine. Salt Lake City: Deseret Book 1970.

Smith, Joseph Fielding, Teachings of the Prophet Joseph Smith. Salt Lake City: Deseret Book 1993.

Snow, Lorenzo, Teachings of the Church: Lorenzo Snow. Salt Lake City: The Church of Jesus Christ of Latter-day Saints. 2012.

Tagore, Rabindranath, Stray Birds. New York: The Macmillan Company 1916.

Talmage, James, Articles of Faith. Salt Lake City: The Deseret News 1899.

The Doctrine and Covenants, "Explanatory Introduction."

Tillman, Charles D., "Unanswered Yet." 1883.

Uchtdorf, Dieter F., "You Are My Hands." General Conference. April 2010.

Uchtdorf, Dieter F., "Continue in Patience." Ensign. May 2010.

vonSchlegel, Katharina, "Be Still My Soul." Hymns of The Church of Jesus Christ of Latter-day Saints. Salt Lake City: The Church of Jesus Christ of Latter-day Saints 1985.

Walker, William R., "Live True to the Faith." General Conference. April 2014.

Whetten, Robert J., "Strengthen Thy Brethren." General Conference. April 2005.

Wilcox, Brad, The Continuous Conversion. Salt Lake City: Deseret Book 2013.

Wirthlin, Joseph B., "Living Water to Quench Spiritual Thirst." General Conference. April 1995.

Wirthlin, Joseph B., "The Virtue of Kindness." General Conference. April 2005.

Wirthlin, Joseph B., Finding Peace in Our Lives. Salt Lake City: Deseret Book 1995.